Sociocybernetics

Sociocybernetics

An actor-oriented social systems approach

Vol. 1

Edited by

R. Felix Geyer,
Netherlands Universities'
Joint Social Research Centre, Amsterdam

Johannes van der Zouwen
Free University, Amsterdam

Martinus Nijhoff Social Sciences Division
Leiden|Boston|London 1978

ISBN-13: 978-90-207-0854-7 e-ISBN-13: 978-1-4613-4095-9
DOI: 10.1007/ 978-1-4613-4095-9

Sole Distributors for North America
Kluwer Boston, Inc.
160 Old Derby Street
Hingham, MA 02043 USA

Preface

The fifteen papers comprising this book were chosen out of the sixty-one contributions to the Symposium and Section on Social Systems held in the context of the Fourth International Congress of Cybernetics and Systems (Amsterdam, The Netherlands, 21-25 August, 1978). These papers, assembled here on the basis of their topicality, depth and originality, cover a wide range of problems, ranging from 'Societies and Turing machines' to 'Dialectics and catastrophe'. An interesting array of themes is considered by authors from six countries. It is felt that these papers, some of them thought-provoking and of great merit, will cast new light on social problems. Though the contributions consider a wide variety of topics, the underlying trend is apparent in many instances.

Of special value is the discussion of the relevance of cybernetics and systems to a wide spectrum of social problems. I think the treatment and the approach adopted by the contributors merit wide attention, since their contributions constitute an appreciable advance in a fairly novel field.

J. ROSE
BLACKBURN (U.K.) May, 1978

Acknowledgements

First of all, we want to thank the authors for their contributions to these volumes, often produced under severe time pressure.

We are particularly indebted to publisher Hans van der Sluijs and desk editor Judy Marcure for their helpful cooperation in having both volumes edited and published on schedule.

We also want to acknowledge the cooperation of the Netherlands Universities' Joint Social Research Centre and the Free University, both in Amsterdam, who granted us administrative assistance and the time to fulfil our editorial duties.

Moreover, we have highly appreciated the feedback received from the members of the Working Group on Social Systems of the Dutch Society for General Systems Research.

Finally, we want to express our gratitude to Dr. J. Rose, the organizer of the congress for which these contributions were written, for his stimulating advice and his willingness to write the preface for this book.

The editors

Contents

List of contributors

PROFESSOR THOMAS BAUMGARTNER, Economy and Society, Institute of Economic Science, Catholic University of Louvain, Rue des Wallons 29, 1348 Louvain-la-Neuve, Belgium.

PROFESSOR JAMES R. BENIGER, Department of Sociology, 2-N-2 Green Hall, Princeton University, Princeton, N.J. 08540, U.S.A.

DR. DON M. M. BOOKER, Visiting Assistant Professor, Department of Systems Analysis, Miami University, 118 East Chestnut Street, Oxford, Ohio 45056, U.S.A.

PROFESSOR TOM R. BURNS, Scandinavian Institutes of Administrative Research, Lund, Sweden, and Institute of Sociology, University of Oslo, Blindern, Box 1096, Oslo 3, Norway.

PROFESSOR PHILIPPE DEVILLÉ, Institute of Economic and Social Research, Catholic University of Louvain, Rue des Wallons 29, 1348 Louvain-la-Neuve, Belgium; Visiting Professor, Department of Economic Sciences, University of Montreal, Canada.

WIL DIJKSTRA, Psychologist, Department of Research Methods, Free University, De Boelelaan 1115, Amsterdam, Netherlands.

PROFESSOR MYRNA L. ESTEP, College of Multidisciplinary Studies, Division of Education, University of Texas at San Antonio, San Antonio, Texas 78285, U.S.A.

PROFESSOR RICHARD L. HENSHEL, Department of Sociology, University of Western Ontario, London N6A 5C2, Ontario, Canada.

DR. BOBBIE J. JONES, Systems Science Center, University of Louisville, Louisville, Kentucky 40208, U.S.A.

PROFESSOR NIKLAS LUHMANN, Fakultät für Soziologie, Universität Bielefeld, Universitätsstrasse, 4800 Bielefeld 1, F.R.G.

PROFESSOR MARIAN MAZUR, Institute of Political Science, Polish Academy of Sciences, Nowy Swiat 47a m.4, 00-042 Warszawa, Poland.

PROFESSOR JAMES G. MILLER, President and Director of Systems Science Center, University of Louisville, Louisville, Kentucky 40208, U.S.A.

PROFESSOR MARIA NOWAKOWSKA, Institute of Philosophy and Sociology, Polish Academy of Sciences, Warszawa, Poland.

LIST OF CONTRIBUTORS

PROFESSOR GORDON PASK, Department of Cybernetics, Brunel University, and Institute of Educational Technology, Open University; Director, System Research Ltd., Woodville House, 37 Sheen Road, Richmond, Surrey TW9 1AJ, England.

PROFESSOR ANATOL RAPOPORT, Department of Psychology, University of Toronto, 11 Saint George Street, Toronto M5S 1A1, Ontario, Canada.

PROFESSOR HERBERT A. SIMON, Department of Psychology and Computer Science, Carnegie Mellon University, Schenley Park, Pittsburgh, Pennsylvania 15213, U.S.A.

PROFESSOR JOHANNES VAN DER ZOUWEN, Department of Research Methods, Free University, De Boelelaan 1115, Amsterdam, Netherlands.

PROFESSOR MARTIN ZWICK, Systems Science Ph.D. Program, Portland State University, P.O. Box 751, Portland, Oregon 97207, U.S.A.

Introduction

R. Felix Geyer and Johannes van der Zouwen

Common themes

The papers brought together in these volumes represent a selection from the more than fifty contributions presented in the symposium and the section on social systems of the Fourth International Congress of Cybernetics and Systems (Amsterdam, August 1978). They cover a wide variety of apparently unrelated topics, and seem to be bound together mainly by their use of the common conceptual framework of sociocybernetics, or social systems theory: indeed, they were all selected for their quality and originality rather than for their mutual fit or for their illustration or observance of a common theme.

Even for the editors themselves, it was therefore surprising and interesting that, on closer inspection, a number of mutually interlocking common themes do emerge. These themes may be described as refutations of the frequently voiced objections against the applications of systems theory to the social sciences (e.g. implicit conservatism, technocratic bias, and unwarranted reductionism). But they can also – and more positively – be viewed as aspects of the emerging 'new cybernetics'. This 'new cybernetics' and its application to social systems can be characterized by the following developments (see also Bråten, 1978):

1. It stresses and gives an epistemological foundation for science as an *observer-dependent* activity. The feedback and feedforward loops characterizing the 'circular' form of systems thinking are not only constructed between the objects observed but also between them and the observer. The subjective character of knowledge is emphasized by this approach: information is neither seen as inherently 'out there' in the observer's environment, nor is it entirely viewed as a figment of his own imagination or a resultant of his own inner cognitive processes. Information is constructed – and continually reconstructed – by the individual in open interaction with his environment. The papers by Pask and Estep illustrate this trend.

2. Modern cybernetics makes it possible to bridge what one might call the 'micro-macro gap' – the gap in social science thinking between the individual and society, between freedom and determinism, between 'anascopic' explanations of society, departing from the activities of individuals conceived as goal-seeking, self-regulating systems, and 'katascopic' explanations, which view society 'from the top down' and see individuals as subservient to system-level criteria for system stability. Baumgartner's actor-oriented systems analysis, Beniger's synthesis of the system and action approaches, and Nowakowska's theory of social change are good examples here.
3. The transition from classical to modern cybernetics is characterized by a number of interrelated *problem shifts*:
   a. One shift is from the system that is being controlled to the actively steering system and consequently (1) to the nature and genesis of the norms on which steering decisions are based, (2) to the information-transformations, based on both observations and norms, that are necessary to arrive at steering decisions, and (3) to the learning processes behind repeated decision-making.
   b. Especially when several systems try to steer each other, or an outside system, attention is focused on the nature of, and the possibilities for, communication or dialogue *between* these systems; it is no accident that studies of artificial intelligence devote so much attention to this communication problem and that questions regarding cooperation or conflict between steering systems become important.
   c. When the behavior of a system has been explained in the classical way, through environmental influences and systemic structure, the problem is raised of the 'why' of this structure itself, qua origin and development, and the 'why' of its autonomy with regard to the environment. In systems terminology: the questions of morphogenesis and autopoiesis.
4. These problem shifts in cybernetics involve a thorough *reconceptualization of many all too easily accepted and taken-for-granted concepts,* which yields new notions of stability, temporality, independence, structure vs. behavior, and many other concepts.

Stability, for complex and therefore necessarily open systems, should be conceived of as a dynamic, floating equilibrium, rather than as a static one as the old notion of homeostatic equilibrium implies. Moreover, such systems are not only changed as a result of the interaction with their environment but they also effectuate intra-systemic change themselves through a regular recoding of their experience, precisely in order to safeguard the continuation of their autonomy.

Luhmann deals with the problem of temporality and shows how in complex systems time and complexity reduction are closely interrelated. Pask asserts that the system-cum-environment's a priori independence in classical cybernetics was a definitional artifact, the result of assuming an independent time coordinate – the observer's time – so that behavioral interactions could be assumed *not* to influence the system's structure; in the new cybernetics, however, phenomena like autopoiesis and organizational closure assume an extremely intricate interdependence between system structure and system behavior.

The individual papers

Pask opens this collection of essays with his conversation-theoretic approach to social systems, not only because his contribution is a good example of a new theoretical development within the emerging framework of the new cybernetics, but also and especially because he illustrates in detail the major epistemological foundations that differentiate the new cybernetics from the more classical approaches.

While stressing the advantages of classical cybernetics with its interdisciplinary and holistic perspective, he argues that non-classical cybernetics endows many traditional concepts with novel meaning. In classical cybernetics, as in classical science, the observer has a definitively reserved external role, compared to the participants in his field of study, while in the new cybernetics any of the participants may act conditionally as an external observer – thus making the theory not only relativistic, but also reflective.

In classical cybernetics structure is imputed from without by an external observer who draws the demarcation lines between the systems studied and their environment and also provides them with an independent time coordinate, so that the system's behavior, unless otherwise specified, does not influence its own stucture. In modern cybernetics, system stability is seen as a process termed 'organizational closure' or 'autopoiesis' which produces specific behaviors and reproduces itself as well as the distinctions with the environment that are necessary for its continued operation. In modern cybernetics, behavior and structure are viewed as mutually interdependent and hence not distinct.

Baumgartner, Burns and DeVillé present another example of the new cybernetics and develop a systems theoretic approach which they refer to as actor-oriented systems analysis to indicate both the dialectical relationship existing between social actors and systems and the duality of the human situation: freedom vs. determinism. They try to integrate theories where social actors are viewed as the essential force which structures and restructures social systems and the conditions of human activity, with the more classical social systems theories, based on systems engineering and influenced by the deterministic natural science paradigm, where actors have to follow 'the iron rules of optimal choice theory in a world of constraints over which they lack control'. Thus, they construct linkages between actors and their strategic and decision-making capabilities on the one hand, and social system dynamics and stability on the other hand. They utilize game theory, viewing games as open rather than as closed systems and study game transformation processes where unsatisfactory games, through 'meta-operations', can indeed be restructured by the participants. Their research has focused on the duality of social action – system-maintaining (reproductive) vs. system-changing (transforming) processes. A multi-level hierarchical model of system stability and change is presented, in which structuring is viewed as an operator on processes, functions and relationships generally, rather than on variables. Their conceptual model is then applied to the structuring of conflict and cooperation and of power systems. It stresses the potential of systems to change their own structure: complex systems are rarely stable, and system stability must be explained in the face of ever-present tendencies for structures to reform, change, or evolve; existing institutional arrangements may be reproduced but can also be transformed by often unintended spin-offs and spill-overs.

Baumgartner applies this actor-oriented systems model to an analysis of industrial democracy measures. He uses elements of Marxist as well as non-Marxist theoretical approaches to the analysis of capitalist production processes and reconceptualizes these in terms of the above model, thus clearly demonstrating the existing linkages between the economic, political, and socio-cultural spheres and demonstrating the influence of the educational system in perpetuating the existing arrangements.

The crucial issue in industrial democracy reforms is to what extent they restructure control relationships within the capitalist enterprise and to what extent increased control by workers over their labor and labor process allows them to extend their control and power to other spheres of social life. Baumgartner's assessment is rather pessimistic here: the reproductive potential of the capitalist system is unlikely to be weakened if power redistribution is limited to the process level, as opposed to the redistribution of meta-power (i.e. the power to alter existing power relationships) at the structural level. Nevertheless, industrial democracy measures, though basically to be considered as structure-maintaining changes, may have important effects in different contexts: e.g. by stimulating changes in cultural norms, educational arrangements, etc.

Nowakowska, in her formal theory of social change, presents another example of a theoretical approach that fits well within the domain of the new cybernetics: it is also a non-mechanistic, non-reductionist multi-level approach, linking individual motivations and behavior to macro-social processes in order to explain social change.

Social change is defined as a substantial change in one or more of the seven 'variables' by which a society is defined, these being: S (the total number of people involved), $\mathcal{G}$ (the social groups existing as subsets of S), C (sets of certain goods), f (a particular distribution of goods), Π (a system of preference relations, per individual, over the class of all functions f), R (the set of rules operating within particular groups and constraining their members' behavior), and σ (a binary relation in S, establishing the communication links between members of S).

Pro-social or anti-social behavior of individuals, in a given situation and with respect to a given group, is not viewed as a personality trait, but as caused by a combination of situational, social and psychological factors; as far as psychological factors are concerned, the combination of high vs. low need for acceptance with high vs. low fear of rejection yields four personality types that are linked with a high or low probability of pro- or anti-social behavior.

A closer analysis of C (the sets of goods), in relation to the other variables defining a society, leads to a distinction in infinitely divisible and scarce goods. Infinitely divisible goods form the basis for a formal theory of freedom, which employs the concepts of equality, preference consistency, and admissibility. Especially scarce goods form a basic concept for the construction of a formal theory of alienation, which deals with the strategies of groups monopolizing the distribution of these scarce goods and also with the emergence of counter-monopolies which attempt to block these strategies. Alienation is viewed as a primary source of social change: first in the consciousness domain, and subsequently, when sufficiently strong counter-monopolies have been formed, in the domain of the allocation of goods.

Finally, the theory is applied to communication networks where the dissemination of innovations in a society is postulated to be dependent on the size of the given group and the density of intra-group relations, in such a way that essential qualitative changes in the dissemination of innovations will occur when the density of these relations exceeds a certain limit.

Booker rightly considers the decision-making process one of the most important in social systems. When it involves a large number of decision-makers, who each develop their own preference of a series of alternative choices and subscribe to democratic procedures, the preference ordering of the majority of decision-akers will soon turn out to be intransitive.

This problem, known among others as the Arrow praradox, is denoted in Booker's contributions as the 'cyclical majority problem'. Booker demonstrates that this problem generally cannot be solved, given a finite time for solution, although chances for a solution increase if the preferences of the decision-makers converge; this problem is closely related to Nowakowska's theory, worked out in the foregoing contribution. However, when value systems between or within groups are incompatible – one of the most important sources of social conflict – the problem can only be solved in two ways: (1) by a *reduction* of the number of decision makers and/or alternatives (e.g. through hierarchization of the decisional process); or (2) by *acceptance*, i.e. when a cyclical decision process is considered acceptable, 'normal' behavior of a social system. This vision evidently entails consequences for the modelling of social systems. To paraphrase the title of Booker's contribution: since societies are not Turing machines, they consequently cannot be modelled as finite automata.

Zwick applies catastrophe theory, developed by Thom and Zeeman, to a qualitative reconceptualization of Hegelian and Marxist dialectics. His essay is a good example of our thesis that developments within the broad domain of general systems theory – even when they have *not* come about in close interaction with social science theorizing or fall within the emerging paradigm of the new cybernetics which this interaction has inspired – do not necessarily have a conservative bias when applied to the social sciences but can, instead, be used to illustrate the restructuring capabilities of systems. Also, the utilization of catastrophe theory forms a good illustration of one of the basic advantages of the general systems approach: the creative use of analogies – from different disciplines, problem areas, or hierarchical levels of organization – to reconceptualize problems in another field, thus adding to their perspicacity.

Especially the catastrophes known as the 'cusp' and the 'butterfly' are used to model the three classical dialectical principles: (1) the transformation of quantity into quality; (2) the unity and struggle of opposites; and (3) the negation of negation. As Zwick himself cautions: 'the catastrophe-theoretic interpretation does not add new content to the Marxian analyses, but merely highlights their underlying coherence, via a rich system of visual metaphor. That is, like dialictics, catastrophe theory provides a language for modeling and a method of exposition'. This, however, is no mean feat by itself; moreover, the possibility of a more quantitative and rigorous use of the theory in the future cannot be excluded. More generally speaking, catastrophe theory seems a promising conceptual tool for modeling any relationship where continuous change in the independent variable results in discontinuous 'jumps' in the dependent one.

In volume 2, *Beniger* – in line with Pask, Baumgartner et al. and Nowakowska – presents yet another theoretical approach which illustrates the diversity of theoretical advances within the new cybernetics. Like Baumgartner et al., he distinguishes two fundamentally different types of social theory: the autonomous system and the purposive action approaches. These are different in their concept of control: in action theories, actors control events to further self-interests; in system theories, causal interactions are maintained by autonomous control relationships. Beniger tries to develop a control theory that integrates these two viewpoints and can be used for the explanation of social change. His generalized concept of control rests on the imagery of flows, both of socially-valued or processed commodities and of information about them. He tries to bridge what we have called earlier the micro-macro gap by answering the crucial question inherent in the system and action approaches taken together: i.e. how do individual actions aggregate in the control patterns required of a social system and how do control systems communicate the requisite patterns of behavior to individual actors.

Individual actors pursue commodities which constitute generalized media of exchange, i.e. media that translate status and rewards across organizational boundaries, which stimulates commodity flows on the action level. On the other hand, the movement of commodities is also regulated by system-wide norms (i.e. the prevailing rules at decision nodes governing the flow of commodities); flows inappropriate to system control will overburden or underutilize system capabilities, which causes normative strain and results in change among actors supplying commodity flows.

Beniger applies his theory to a recent example of social change, the rapid rise in illegal drug use, and analyzes the flows of commodities (referrals of drug users) and information between the educational, legal, and medical institutions concerned with the problem. Out of twelve possible flows between these three types of institutions, four are predominant: user referrals from the educational to the medical and legal spheres, and drug-related information in the opposite directions. Referral flows are put in motion, on the demand side, by specialists who seek media to translate individual status and rewards *across* organizational boundaries and, on the supply side, by non-specialists who seek competent assistance in a specialized area. A rapid rise in the number of drug users causes normative strain and results in a liberalization of the customary definition of deviance. Several hypotheses pertaining to normative strain are formulated.

Mazur, though not working within the framework of the new cybernetics, presents an interesting illustration of how much can be done with only a minimum of systems theoretical concepts, provided they are applied consistently. With the aid of a simple two-system interaction model and a few concise algebraic equations, he logically deducts a series of theorems about the mutual interdependence of two interacting systems, building one upon the next. Introducing the notion of reactivity (i.e. the ratio of output quantity to input quantity), he relates this notion to the behavior of two interacting systems and to the concepts of (positively or negatively) divergent, stable, and convergent feedback.

Estep exemplifies the work that has been done recently in the social systems field to counter the criticisms against the systems approach as being overly simple, reductionist and mechanistic. She distinguishes three epistemological categories of knowing: quantitative, performative, and qualitative, the latter being defined as consisting of the set of formal epistemological conditions defining *cognitive* sensitive awareness (knowing) of unique properties of persons, events, or objects. She then argues that classical cybernetics cannot be considered sufficiently sophisticated to characterize qualitative knowing, due to the information limitation of these models, and develops a SIGGS information-theoretic characterization of qualitative knowing which includes, as the acronum suggests, elements of Set theory, Information theory, Graph theory, and General Systems theory. Estep further distinguishes and describes three categories of qualitative knowing – recognition, acquaintive qualitative knowing, and appreciative qualitative knowing – and then goes on to describe the SIGGS-theoretic model which contains – in addition to concepts like system, input, output, and feedback – also concepts like feedin, toput, feedout, fromput, and feedthrough. The model is then illustrated by applying it to empirical research among handicapped learners in a classroom setting.

Dijkstra and *Van der Zouwen* apply systems methodology to the intricacies of interviewer-respondent interaction in survey research and develop a black box model of the interview process. They distinguish three possible respondent roles: the faithful, the good, and the ingratiating respondents, and argue that normally the respondent effectuates a role compromise between these three basic orientations. This role compromise will be different in each concrete case and depends on, among other things, the respondent's role conception, and on role inducement (defined by the interview situation and, more specifically, by the way the respondent is explicitly or implicitly cued by the interviewer). A weighted response function is developed which reckons with the respondent's uncertainties and incorporates weighted estimates of the contribution of each of the three basic orientations to the respondent's answer. Eight propositions regarding respondent behavior result in nine equations, formulated in an empirically testable form. In a special section on the plausibility and applicability of the model, results from two types of studies (accuracy studies and covariance studies) are presented, which help to further refine the model presented. Finally, prescriptions to reduce biasing effects in the interview situation are derived from the model.

Jones and *Miller*, although operating within the framework of classical cybernetics, show the usefulness of this approach in their cross-level analysis of alteration of information in channels. Using insights more fully developed in Miller's recent book, *Living systems*, they distinguish seven hierarchical levels of living systems, characterized by increasing complexity: cell, organ, organism, group, organization, society and supra-national system. Each system, regardless of its level of complexity, has to carry out 19 different processes if it is to survive (e.g. intake and storage of information).

The potential fertility and unifying power of the classical general systems approach are demonstrated by its capacity to generate cross-level hypotheses, making use of analogies in processes at different hierarchical levels of complexity. In this particular case, a hypothesis about information degradation in channels is presented as a derivation of the Second Law of Thermodynamics, and is described especially at the level of the group and the level of society, with regard to the spread of rumors. Three stages in the transmission of rumors are discerned: leveling, sharpening, and assimilation. These are illustrated by presenting and reinterpreting empirical data from several studies.

Luhmann, after these demonstrations of the applicability of classical general systems theory to the social sciences, can again be considered a representative of the new cybernetics. He directs his analysis specifically to the extreme complexity of social systems, a neglected element in classical systems thinking, and links the problem of complexity to the need for a new conceptualization of time, system-bound rather than defined by an external observer, and intimately related to the concepts of organizational closure and self-referencing, recently developed within the systems paradigm.

Extremely complex systems can no longer relate all their elements, as simpler systems still can. The structure of complex systems is precisely the result of a selective process that results in a *limited* interdependence of elements. In the theory of social systems, time has been dealt with mainly from the viewpoint of stability and is measured by system-external criteria (e.g. the observer's clocks). However, in a complex and fluctuating environment, complex systems can only maintain themselves as dynamic systems which can change their own structures in order to adapt to changing environmental conditions: by being able to change the interrelations between their elements over time, complex systems are not committed to a simple pattern of interconnectivity, and thus can actualize more relations sequentially than would be possible simultaneously.

Time compensates for the disadvantages of size, and for the problem of selection which increases overproportionally with size. Time-bound or 'temporalized' systems can only consist of time-bound elements, or events. This goes especially for social systems, the ultimate elements of which are specific events or actions: no action can be constituted without system and no system is imaginable without actions. Events are defined by the actuality of change; the measurement of time, not required for their identification as such, is nevertheless necessary to separate events from states – i.e. past events, coded in memory.

Luhmann – like Baumgartner, Nowakowska and Beniger – bridges the micro-macro gap between large-scale systems and the actors operating within them by pointing to the linkage functions that can be ascribed to actions: (1) depending on the intended or ascribed meaning of an action, certain other actions become more or less probable; and (2) the meaning that is attributed to series of interactions makes time individual-independent through here-and-now communication. Communication allows one to share the sequencing of events within one's own individual time horizon with others, so that quasi-simultaneous events melt together and an intersubjectively shared time horizon emerges. Time thus becomes a culturally interpretable dimension of the world: socialization serves the generalization of time and therewith a further enlargement of relational possibilities.

Luhmann stresses the processual character of systems, and argues that process should not be defined as a basic concept, but that the classical notion of process should be reinterpreted as a combinatory effort of a system that has to temporalize its elements and therefore has to attune the relations between these elements to this purpose. Systemic processes are not simply unrelated series of facts; they owe their unity, in spite of temporal distance, to a combination of selectivities, where each event within a process codetermines the selection of the following ones. The author finally presents an analysis of the evolution of society since the 16th century in the direction of greater internal complexity, temporalization of time, and institutionalization of self-reflection.

Simon, from a different vantage point than Luhmann, also focuses on the extreme complexity of large-scale social systems. He argues that very large systems, whether natural or man-made, are almost universally hierarchical in structure, since this considerably reduces the time required for their evolution. Hence, they can be partially decomposed, by making subdivisions of weakly interacting blocks of strongly interacting elements. When complex systems are observed over a moderate time span and with some maximum frequency of observation, genuine dynamic behavior can be observed only at the intermediate hierarchical level. At the lowest level, only the equilibrium distributions of the smallest components can be detected, since they interact strongly at high frequency and thus move rapidly toward internal equilibrium. At the highest level, the largest components may appear to be stationary, since the time span of observation is too short to detect aggregate change in them. The simulation of such systems can be greatly simplified by exploiting these properties: the dynamics of behavior at each level can be studied independently by aggregating behavior at the level below and by treating components at the level above as approximately constant.

The emphasis on prediction in macro-social models is misplaced; prediction is impossible due to lack of knowledge of the relevant socio-economic mechanisms, and it is not needed for policy purposes. It is not necessary to forecast the future but to understand the consequences of alternative *possible* futures, and to understand which of these is associated with particular strategies or policy measures.

Rapoport also deals with the simulation of large-scale social systems. Computer simulation, for the social sciences, is not only a substitute for otherwise too complex mathematical deductions as in the natural sciences but also a substitute for the lack of a real laboratory for large-scale systems. However, there is a feedback between the research technology employed (e.g. computer simulation) and the direction research takes, which should be carefully monitored, because it implies a tendency for the researcher to be fixated on concepts that are easy to operationalize for that particular technology, while these concepts subsequently help to shape the researcher's image of reality. The dangers inherent in this are illustrated by a discussion of a mathematical model of arms control. If the assumptions that go into a model are incorrect, this will not only result in unrealistic predictions, but it will also tend to *create* reality, especially in the case of complex models of large-scale systems. The power game model, for example, tends to become self-fulfilling; the 'reality' of the power structure is entirely generated in the minds of men and stems from its acceptance. Likewise, however, a more positive feedback between model and reality might be established, e.g. in simulations of the conditions for an improvement of the quality of life.

Henshel, like Rapoport, deals with the relationship between science and its environment – in this case not the interaction between the scientist's models and reality, but the deviation-amplifying feedback between the prestige of a discipline and the accuracy of its social predictions.

Henshel specifically investigates the effects of predictor prestige on predictive accuracy. He considers it self-evident that the accuracy of scientific predictions influences the prestige of the discipline which issues them, and he devotes his essay to the opposite problem – i.e. to an analysis of the different ways in which a discipline's prestige may influence its predictive power. He argues that in most 'prestige loops', which include disciplinary prestige and predictive power as elements, the signs of the relationships are all positive, so that deviation-amplifying mutual causal feedback occurs: small changes may accumulate through several 'trips' around a feedback loop.

One type of prestige loop occurs through dispersion of the disciplinary perspective among the members of a society. A discipline with sufficient prestige can eventually shape the institutional forms of its subject matter and may so far permeate the thinking of the subject that many of its postulates appear obvious a priori. Examples are given from economics, IQ-testing and Freudian psychology.

Another type of prestige loop, especially in case of concrete predictions about specific events, is characterized by 'negative feedback': it has built-in mechanisms which *inhibit* the growth of prestige and accuracy.

Self-altering prophecies, both of the self-fulfilling and self-defeating variety, are all the more interesting when they are issued by social science itself. When prophecies are deemed credible, alterable, and important, people may take individual or concerted action to level or improve its chances, thus altering their accuracy and therewith the prestige of the predictor. When social science prophecies are heeded and generally become self-defeating, social science should decline in respect. Since predictions will no longer be listened to, their accuracy will consequently rise again, leading in turn to a rise in social science prestige, whereupon the cycle is repeated in a continuous process. However, when social science prophecies become self-fulfilling (as they generally are when the predicted state is desirable, and/or when selfish rather than concerted action is predominant), a multiplier effect occurs as can be observed, for example, in the field of election polling.

Henshel quotes Sjoberg and Nett as saying that the most effective forecaster might be the man who was right 60 or 70 percent of the time, and he ends with the intriguing conclusion that the social sciences can conceivably alter their own accuracy and prestige by a judicious selection or withholding of predictions.

Although we have not ventured into predictions, it is hoped that the essays presented in these volumes will enhance the accuracy and prestige of sociocybernetics.

Reference:

Bråten, Stein, 'Systems research and social sciences,' in: G. J. Klir (ed.), *Applied general systems research: recent developments and trends*, New York, Plenum Press, 1978, 655-685.

A conversation theoretic approach to social systems*

Gordon Pask

There is a deplorable tendency in contemporary thinking to trivialise the content of deep and fascinating areas of knowledge.

By way of illustration, this tendency is manifest in psychology as a systematic down rating of 'psychology' to read '*a* psychology' (i.e. one or another, preferably easy-to-deal with, school of thought *about* the subject); it does not matter *which* one, it might be behaviourism, or one of the psychoanalytic schools, or 'explanation by artificial intelligence', (alias, in some quarters, 'cognitive science'). Maybe the tendency in question is born of mental laziness, maybe fear of being mistaken, maybe (but I do not really believe this) sheer inability to reason globally without recourse to vague and often vacuous ideas (which are frequently cited, later on, as good evidence that any other-than-particular mode of reasoning is unscientific). The result, at any rate, is to demean the several schools of thought by presenting hypotheses, data, etc., that are very safe and sure about very small issues.

So, for example, 'psychology' (in contrast to '*a* psychology' which may, legitimately, rest on any sensibly chosen postulates) deals, even in its dictionary definition, with consciousness. It must question the fashionable assumptions about time and independence – borrowed from classical mechanics, where they prove outstandingly successful – since, if you take the trouble to look at psychological happenings, these assumptions are seldom successful and often positively fatuous. It must examine the notion of individuality, and so on.

'Mainstream' psychology does none of these things because it is not 'psychology' at all but a mixture of 'schools of psychology', some of which take consciousness for granted, some of which do not mention it, some of

* The views expressed in this paper are based upon research supported by SSRC Research Programme HR 2708/2: Learning Styles, Educational Strategies, and Representations of Knowledge: Methods and Applications, by Grant AFOSR 78-3520: (Engineering Design) through the European Office, Grant DAERO 76 G 069: (Principles of Decision) through the European Office, and carried out at System Research Ltd.

which regard it as irrelevant (some, too, that naively identify this commodity with certain neural excitations that are positively correlated with the conscious state). All of the current schools take time (meaning, the point-interval convention of Newtonian physics), as the one and only *given* metric of process. Why, heaven knows, for I can find no other-than-tendentiously obtained results to justify this cavalier treatment, nor, for example, can Atkin (1977). Independence is commonly assumed to exist where it is *convenient* for it to exist, in order to apply the most elegant statistical techniques. Hence, as often as not, statistical analyses simply buttress the 'respectability' of work, rather than yielding, as they *could* and *should* do, valuable condensations and comparisons of data. Regarding individuality (the last of the specific issues under discussion), there is an intriguing subculture of double-talk, whereby individuality is on the one hand learned or acquired (yet regarded as a right, not a privilege) and on the other hand unquestioningly assigned to distinct (biological) organisms (yet these organisms are said to form a society). The ethos is quaint, to say the least of it. But the underlying ratiocination is not the stuff of science.

A very similar tendency influences work in the social sciences, sociology, education, social anthropology, forecasting, economic theory, and the rest. The degeneration of psychology has been rhetorically chastised because it is a social science with which I am familiar and, with Lewis, have recently completed an historical survey of 'problem solving' (Pask, 1978). In that field, at any rate, the degenerative mechanisms stand out as obtrusive, but 'mainstream' psychology is probably no more culpable in this respect than any other 'mainstream' discipline.

Cybernetics (equisignificantly, *General System Theory*), is an interdisciplinary science – and thus a science which must heed the foundations of the disciplines it relates, explains, or unifies. It might be expected to remedy the omissions, to untie the knots of confusion, and to repair the defects we have just examined. Its record is not of outstanding success; perhaps because we, as practitioners, are too diffident in questioning the great unquestionables.

To place the matter in perspective, there is a classical and a non-classical brand of Cybernetics (General System Theory) and both of them are of value in their place. As sciences, they are both interdisciplinary and thoroughly committed to a holistic, though rigorous, vision of things. The classical variety, however, deviates minimally, at the foundational level of discourse, from the traditional canons of scientific thinking. The non-classical variety replaces the traditional ideas of stability, structure, behaviour, temporality, independence and (where relevant) consciousness, by notions that are more complex and broadly conceived, that do not contradict, but may encompass, the traditional norms.

Where, in classical science, the observer has a definitely *reserved* external role, in the non-classical theory he is on a par with the participants in the system, any of whom may step outside the system to act conditionally as external observers.

It is here that the classical paradigms break down. All science is relativistic, namely, to the one or several point(s) of view of an external observer who determines, by his perspective(s), the frame of reference relative to which events occur. The more restrictive dogmas reserve a special canonical reference frame, which has a particular usefulness in studies either of particulate phenomena or gross phenomena, but is otherwise limited to observations of one kind of event (one universe of interpretation).

Even classical cybernetics admits several perspectives and, insofar as it is genuinely interdisciplinary (rather than merely coursing through the universes proper to several disciplines), several perspectives are simultaneously maintained. Hence, the notion of relativism is more complex there than it is, for example, in mechanics or elementary physics. However, the main point of departure comes when the curiously reserved position of an external observer is relinquished, and the theory becomes not only relativistic but *reflective*, also. Each possible observer (in social systems each possible participant, role, school of thought, culture, society, institution, etc.) may have its own class of perspectives. As a result, we must seriously countenance the integrity and individuality of these perspective-having entities, the reality of speaking to them as 'You', and 'I', rather than 'it', or 'that'. A rigorous, quantifiable, yet subjective, (insofar as 'objective' literally implies 'it-referenced'), theory is required.

Conversation Theory (Lewis and Pask 1965; Pask 1972, 1975a, b, 1976a, b, c, 1977a, b, 1978; Pask and Scott 1972, 1973; Pask, Scott and Kallikourdis 1973, 1975) is an attempt to provide such a vehicle. It carries with it novel methods of measurement, both sharp valued and fuzzy.

The basic tenet of the theory is that the minimal, psychologically realistic, organisation which is susceptible to sharp valued measurement is a conversation in a language L between participants A and B. Sharp valued observations are made of L conversational events. Quite often A and B can be safely (but loosely) identified with people. They are actually specified (in the theory) as *coherent and stable conceptual systems*. So, for example, if it is possible to isolate distinct perspectives adopted by one person (and it is, using proper means to exteriorise a normally hidden conceptual process), then Conversation Theory deals with 'Conversations' that are normally 'internal to one person's brain', between perspectives A and B. At the other end of the spectrum, stable conceptual systems not uncommonly exist in several, maybe many, brains over which they are distributed, (cultures, schools of thought, traditions, social institutions). Hence, cultures A and B may 'converse', or people may converse with cultures, and so on.

Conversation Theory thus *socializes man* (*either in a conversation 'with himself', with some others, or 'with society'*). In this respect it is adapted to the position of Valosinov (1976: p. 11) which he phrases, most succinctly, in accepting the Socratic dictum 'man is an animal' *if*, and only if, 'man is a *social* animal'.

To some extent, the social character of the theory has been overlooked, at any rate not fully exploited, partly as a result of its application. The theory has been applied, for the most part, in studies of education, learning, design, '*creativity*' (or 'originality' in Liam Hudson's (1978) sense) theory building, knowledge representation, decision making by groups and individuals, and the resolution of problematic situations. Although all these intellectual or concrete activities have a social component, they are usually regarded as lying within the province of psychology, or epistemology, or behavioural studies.

As will be seen, Conversation Theory involves various subtheories, to do with *analogical reasoning* and information regarded as a degree of consciousness, with a content that amounts to procedures shared between the entities A and B that are, in the conversational (social) process, conscious (that *are* conscious beings, not simply are *regarded* as conscious beings). This leads, in turn, to a reformulation of nearly all notions to do with stability, temporality, independence, as well as the traditional demarcation of a 'structure' and a 'behaviour' of the process, social or otherwise, said to have this structure.

Let me illustrate this point, so that we are clear about the kind of departure made. In *classical cybernetics*, it is assumed that a system can (somehow) be demarcated from its environment. *How* is left to the common sense, or the conventional wisdom, of an external observer, with reserved status. He chooses dimensions or coordinates, restricted to adumbrate a structure, in which trajectories represent behaviours; either deterministic behaviours of a system with instantaneous states, or the probabilistic behaviours of an ensemble. If the trajectories converge to a fixed point, or a limit cycle, to which they return after small, but arbitrary, perturbation, then the system is equilibrially, or dynamically, stable. With ingenuity, all manner of adaptation and the like can be accommodated – by attaching parameters to families of state spaces, or by similar expedients – without changing the fundamental picture. It should be added, parenthetically, that the picture employs the trick of assuming an independent time coordinate (the time of an external observer), so that trajectories (behaviours) in the space do not, unless the contrary is preordained, influence the structure imposed upon it (due to which the system-environment complex can itself be deemed '*a priori* independent' of other systems, or the external observer who obtains 'information' from the system).

In *non-classical cybernetics*, the situation is different. A scheme of productions is postulated, such that these are candidate operations for being (a) *productive* and (b) *reproductive* in respect of some arguments (some substrate or medium).

A system is stable, insofar as there is a process (not a reserved time sequence) such that the productions are executed, and, amongst other things, reproduce themselves and the distinctions that structure the substrate, or medium, required for their execution, i.e. the neural, chemical, electronic, etc., medium, inhabited by the process that executes or realises the production scheme as coherent activity. Such criteria of stability are called '*organisational closure*' by Varela (1975), Varela and Goguen (1976), or (for biological embodiments) '*Autopoiesis*', by Maturana and Varela (1976) and are identical with *P Individualisation* and *conceptual stability* in (my own) Theory of Conversations (Pask 1976b, c, 1977a, b).

The production scheme may be viewed as a syntax of a language, L; its realisation calls for a many-sorted logic of processors (or coherent event-sets, not simply sets of static elements), as the semantic interpretation of stable (syntactic) expressions.

Notice that a system in a language, L, which is stable by organisational closure, is (usually) informationally open, (because its productions do more than 'reproduce', in the trivial sense of 'replicate'). Further, information transfer acquires a fundamental, rather than purely metrical, significance (Petri, 1965; Holt, 1972), i.e. the coming about of dependency between *a priori* independent organisationally closed units or equisignificantly between *a priori* asynchronous units, each unit being a process.

In conversation theory, where the units are social entities like people, factions, points of view, groups, it is usual to add a further stipulation, i.e. to credit the language, L, with a complete semiotic by adjoining a pragmatic component (any unit has a non-trivial intention, or purpose). That is, any unit may see or be seen from several perspectives; there is no unit which, except by volition, has but one perspective, nor can any unit exist in isolation. This statement is compatible with the proper formalisation of the theory undertaken by Gergely, Nemeti and their colleagues (1977), and also with the representations of Von Foerster (1976), Glanville (1976), Varela (1975) and Maturana (1976).

Within the non-classical paradigm, the behaviour makes the structure, and vice versa; hence, they are not distinct. *Information transfer* becomes *dependency-occurrence*, manifest as *consciousness*. Time emerges, insofar as a perspective is adopted by at least one stable participating unit, and is a particular representation of process (see Bykhovsky (1974), Gaines (1976, 1977), or Milne and Milner (1977)). Classical stability is a special and seldom encountered, limiting-case of organisational closure (the non-classical criterion of stability).

A conversation is an information transfer, between units *A*, *B*..., involving the exchange of procedures (i.e. executable production schemes), such that a further organisational closure is obtained. I generally refer to minimal units as '*stable concepts*'; and participants *A* and *B* are, typically, made up of many. Such an exchange, which I call an 'understanding', is the least sharp valued observable for an external observer* (one of the participants, like *A*, *B*..., perhaps) who desires a full ordering of understandings, in his time structure. The information transfer is the degree of *A*'s consciousness with *B* (or *B*'s with *A*) of whatever coherent procedures are exchanged to secure and stabilise an understanding regarding these procedures that achieve (say) a concept for topic *T*. The content of this consciousness is the set of procedures shared by *A* and *B*; the local synchronicity (alias, dependency) which is required for coherent execution induces a common element in the time of *A* and *B*, from the perspectives they adopt to engage in (verbal or non verbal) discourse regarding *T*.

There is a trick in the non-classical theory, also. Participants have agreed beliefs, which may be formalised as *coherence truths*. Agreements refer to concepts of many kinds, tautological and abstract, or analogical.

If a participant elects to act as an external observer, then he also desires to assert a *veridicial truth*, but in some metalanguage, L^*, over the conversational language, L.

What kind of L^* statement is the minimal veridicial truth he can assert? It is not a proposition. It is a metaphor, designating an analogy, '*A* and *B* agree over an understanding of *T*' in which the similarity (agreement over *T*) is

* Sharp valued observations usually, in fact commonly, are surrounded by sets of Fuzzy observables.

supported by a distinction between A and B (at most A's concept of T is isomorphic to B's concept of T, they are not, by definition, identical).

Is Conversation Theory (or some non-classical, relativistic, and reflective theory, akin to it) necessary and desirable as the basis for social science? I am persuaded that it is, partly on aesthetic grounds, and out of scientific disposition, but also for practical reasons. Classical theories, even Cybernetic ones, do not appear to work (unless they are propped up by *meta-theoretic assumptions* which, in the interests of mental hygiene, should be made explicit *in* the theory of social science) and there are some sound arguments to suggest that they cannot work, in principle.

There is, at one extreme, a form (or perhaps a parody) of social science, pervasive in mainstream economics and demography, which uses the reserved position of a classical external observer to ordain that men are 'economic men', or 'welfare men', or whatever. The external observer is *not* such a thing, himself, and recognises that his model is a gross approximation to the nature of man. When questioned on this score, either by default, in regulating a social system, by his own conscience, or by peer criticism, he relegates the issue of what man *is* to another discipline, psychology. This expedient is futile since it was noted previously (albeit, in the crudest outline) that mainstream psychology plays exactly the same trick (either the nature of man is passed on to the biologists, thence to the molecular biologists, thence to the biochemists, etc., or else it is returned to the social sciences, when the cycle is immediately tautologous). Probably the most damage is done by the compelling simplicity of (for example) an 'economic' or an 'avaricious' image of man at the microlevel of game theoretic, or decision theoretic formulations. Manifestly, game theory, except in the sense of Homo Ludens (Huizinga, 1949) which is not at all the intended sense, is inapplicable to most social transactions, and although Howard (1966, 1971) tries to remedy the matter with metagame theory, the mathematical apparatus obfuscates the attempt to image such realities as mutual anticipation and hypothesis testing (see the debate on this issue between Howard, (1976) Rapoport (1976), and Robinson (1976a)). But, even on the large scale, the employment of a 'man as an object' model is misleading at the turning point, where human concern, and human interest, come into the picture, i.e. where economics, the dynamics of transportation, or whatever, becomes a *social* science.

True, there are macroscopic theories, epitomised by the work of Forrester (1973), Meadows (1974) and Mesarovic (1972), which have much greater legitimacy. The case for and against these global modelling approaches is surveyed, in a masterly fashion, by Clark and Cole (1975). As a personal comment, I am not too much impressed by Forrester's addition of Chapter 8 ('physical versus social limits') to 'World Dynamics', in order to redress the balance in favour of the social issues at stake; nor is Fig. 8.1 of that book a very convincing depiction of how society might react. The legitimacy stems, to my mind, from retaining the gist of an original intention; the 'Club of Rome' saw the computer as a 'public relations' device. Rightly so, and not trivially, either; it is used as a means of publically displaying complex, non-linear, imaginations.

These computer programmed models are macro-level classical cybernetics, *par excellence.* The difficulties occasioned by employing a classical approach are more readily noted in the relatively detailed study of smaller social systems; for example, Bateson's (1958) examination of the Naven ritual or the cultural 'double bind' or the work by Rapaport (1968) on ritual regulation or, on cargo cultures and similar messianic movements, by Schwartz (1962), Festinger (1972) or by Barnett (1977). There are parallels, in the regulation of animal communities discussed by Wynne Edwards (1963) (who drew from and acknowledged the inspiration of Carr Saunders, 1922), and in Tyler Bonner (1958) (as a theorist of evolution) or Waddington (1957) (of embryology).

The trouble is that, on close examination, Rapaport's Tsembaga 'ritual cycle' is *not* accommodated in the classical framework, since tribal structure depends upon behaviour; by the same token, the 'cultural double bind' relies upon a social contract which is inexpressible (Robinson (1976a, b)) without the stability criterion of organisational closure, as Bateson (1973) surely agrees.

If that is so, then Conversation Theory appears to be a sensible candidate for the most apposite social theory.

Conversation Theory is by no means original in intent. It underpins the *epistemology* of Vygotsky (1962) and, in a different but compatible domain, Piaget (1968). In the context of realistically larger social organisations its ideas stand out from Moscovici's (1976) theory; it is latent in the existential transactionalism of Buber (1958) and the heterarchical transactionalism summarised and developed by Burns (1976) in his discussion of social dialectic. With greater precision, Bråten (1977) develops a full theory, with Herbst (1976). Bråten's (independent) theory affirms my conviction that Conversation Theory is a viable proposition in the social sciences for which it may do, as it has done for some areas of psychology, the job of firming up complex but often loosely stated paradigms.

Theory formulation is a matter of taste. I favour Schumacher (1973), Barzun (1964) or Lakatos (1973) with their optimism, Illich (1973) in his constructive mood; the traditions which embody the content of many an age. I am frightened by the well-intentioned pessimism of Ellul (1965) or Heilbronner (1975) or Toffler (1970). But that provokes me to do something about it. For example, Vickers' (1970) elegant system theoretic concept of 'Social Appreciation' should be rendered fully operational.

Conversation Theory provides (if it is wanted) the sharp valued quantification of a science. It can be expressed, perhaps with less precision, but with principles unchanged, in the large; to accommodate systems of the scale considered by Beer (1974). Some relevant studies are due to Robinson (1976) and Ben Eli (1976).

There is a real (but, I believe, unjustified) anxiety that the large scale implementation of conversation theoretic techniques will boil down to something reminiscent of a 'global model' simulation. The anxiety is most often expressed by people who are struck by the liberal use of conversations *through* (it should be emphasised not *with*) computing machinery as the means of achieving a series of strict laboratory paradigms for teaching/learning or proposing/developing hypotheses. Cursory scrutiny of Lewis and Pask; Pask; Pask and Scott; Pask, Scott and Kallikourdis (ibid.), *does* suggest that the theory is somehow machine bound.

Even if it were, the theory is not irrelevant to the social sciences. Methods of conversation through a mechanical interface, most fitted to one or two subjects, have been extended to small group operation in the *learning/teaching environment* (as reported in Lewis and Pask, 1969) and are currently used in team operation for decision/design environments (including such activities as planning or theory building). In other words, there is no difficulty in going from two-person to several-person interaction, using computers as distributive media and no other-than-technical limitation in contemplating nation-wide or industry-wide systems.

But the fact is, the theory is *not* machine bound. Insofar as hardware is invoked, it is used in a way that is *not* like a simulation (still less a simple computer conferencing network). Moreover, the principles made clear under these circumstances remain if the machinery is replaced by biological and architectural hardware (without denying that computation, in a rather liberal sense, is a valuable and possibly mandatory catalytic agent, to be used as it is needed). Conversation Theory itself is about conceptual processes, about intellect and imagination (*not*, for example, about a non-existent 'pure cognition', nor about a non-existent 'pure knowledge' devoid of a theorist or expositor or progenitor). It *is* concerned with consciousness, it *does* challenge the absolute character of a distinction between an external observer (practitioner) and a participant (a member, or group of members of society), it *does*, for all its insistence upon coherence or agreement support (in fact, demand) a *proper calculus of analogical reasoning*, and forms of abduction or innovation (rather than deduction and induction) akin to the schemes proposed by Koestler (1964) or Schon (1963).

My own criteria are unashamedly aesthetic. Conversation Theory (or any equivalent rival) sets the arid particularity of traditional studies into a more beautiful context. Either it transforms the meaning of 'scientific activity', or (as you prefer it), ushers in an age when 'science' subsumes art and politics, without degrading either personality or the quality of creative action. Many applications are possible in the 'social sciences' or just 'in society'. Current stresses in society encourage the effort to winkle out, and to work out, these applications. This is a great and very exciting enterprise.

References

Atkin, R., *Combinatorial Connectivities in Social Systems*, London: Heinemann, 1977.
Barnett, H. G., *Innovation. The Basis for Cultural Change*, New York: McGraw-Hill, 1977.
Bateson, G., *Steps Towards an Ecology of Mind*, London: Intertext Books, 1972.
Bateson, G., *Naven* (2nd ed.), Stanford, Calif.: Stanford University Press, 1958.
Barzun, J., *Science: The Glorious Entertainment*, London: Seecker and Warburg, 1964.
Beer, S., *Designing Freedom*, New York: Wiley, 1974.
Ben Eli, M., *Comments on the Cybernetics of Stability and Regulation in Social Systems* (Ph.D. thesis), Brunel University, 1976.
Bråten, S., 'The Human Dyad', *Systems and Simulations No. 72*, Institute of Sociology, University of Oslo, 1977.
Buber, M., *I and Thou*, Edinburgh: Edinburgh University Press, 1958.
Burns, T. R., *The Dialectics of Social Systems No 56*, Institute of Sociology, University of Oslo, 1976.
Bykhovsky, V. K., 'Control and Information Processing in Asynchronous Processor Networks', *Proc. Finland USSR Symposium on Micro Processors and Data Processors*, Helsinki, Vol. 1, distributed 1974.
Carr Saunders, A. M., *The Population Problem*, London: Oxford, 1922.
Clark, J. and S. Cole, *Global Simulation Models*, New York: Wiley, 1975.
Ellul, J., *The Technological Society*, London: Jonathan Cape, 1965.
Festinger, L., *Cognitive Dissonance*, Stanford, Cal.: Stanford University Press, 1972.
Forrester, J. W., *World Dynamics*, New York: Wright Allen Press. 1973.
Gaines, B. R., 'Foundations of Fuzzy Reasoning', *Man Machine Systems Laboratory*, University of Essex, 1976.
Gaines, B. R., 'System Identification Approximation and Complexity', *Man Machine Systems Laboratory*, University of Essex, 1977.
Gergely, T. and I. Nemeti, Various 1977 publications, Institute of Applied Computer Science, Hungarian Academy of Science, Budapest.

Glanville, R., 'A Cybernetic Development of Theories of Epistemology and Observation with Reference to Space and Time (as seen in Architecture)'. (Ph.D. Thesis), 1978,Brunel University, 1976.

Herbst, P. G., *Alternatives to Hierarchies*, 1976.

Heilbronner, R. L., *An Inquiry into the Human Prospect*, New York: Calder and Boyars, 1975.

Holt, A., Comments in M. C. Bateson (ed.), *Our Own Metaphor*, New York: A. Knopf, 1972.

Howard, N., 'The theory of metagames', *General Systems Yearbook* 11, 167-186, 1966.

Howard, N., *Paradoxes of Rationality*, Cambridge, Mass.: The M.I.T. Press, 1971.

Howard, N., 'Solution by General Metagames', *Behavioral Science* 21, Nr. 6, 524-532, 1976.

Hudson, L., *Contrary Imaginations*, London: Pelican, 1978.

Huizinga, J., *Homo Ludens*, London: Routledge and Kegan Paul, 1949.

Illich, I., *Deschooling Society*, Harmondsworth: Penguin Books, 1973.

Koestler, A., *The Act of Creation*, London: Hutchinson, 1964.

Lakatos, I., 'History of the Science and its Rational Reconstruction' in *Boston Studies in the Philosophy of Science VIII*, Dordrecht: Reidel (see also in the same volume, criticisms of 'Research Programmes' by Kuhn, Feigel, Hall, Kortge and Lakatos), 1973.

Lewis, B. N. and G. Pask, 'The Theory and Practice of Adaptive Teaching Machines' in R. Glaser (ed), *Teaching Machines and Programmed Learning*, New York: Nat. Educ. Assn. of USA, 1965.

Lewis, B. N. and G. Pask, 'The Self Organisation of a Three Person Task Oriented Group' in *The Simulation of Human Behaviour*, Paris: Dunod 291-311, 19679.

Mesarovic, M. D., 'A Mathematical Theory of General Systems' in G. J. Klir (ed), *Trends in General System Theory*, New York: Wiley, 1972.

Maturana, H. and F. Varela, '*Autopoietic Systems: A Characterisation of the Living Organisation*', BCL Publications on microfiche.

Meadows, D. H. and D. L. Meadows, *The Limits to Growth*, London: Pan Books, 1974.

Milne, G. and R. Milner, 'Concurrent Processes and their Syntax', *Internal Report Computer Science Dept.*, University of Edinburgh.

Moscovici, S., *Social Influence and Social Change*, New York: Academic Press, 1976.

Pask, G., 'A Fresh Look at Cognition and the Individual', *Int. J. Man-Machine Studies* 4, 211-216, 1972.

Pask, G., *The Cybernetics of Human Learning and Performance*, London: Hutchinson, 1975a.

Pask, G., *Conversation, Cognition and Learning*, Amsterdam and New York: Elsevier, 1975b.

Pask, G., 'Conversational Techniques in the Study and Practice of Education' *Brit. J. Educational Psychology* 46, I, 12-25, 1976a.

Pask, G., 'Styles and Strategies of Learning'. *Brit. J. Educational Psychology* 46, II, 128-148, 1976b.

Pask, G., *Conversation Theory: Applications in Education and Epistemology*. Amsterdam and New York: Elsevier, 1976.

Pask, G., 'Organisational Closure of Potentially Conscious Systems'. *Proc.* NATO *Conference on Applied General Systems Research*, with *Notes and additions. Realities Conference* EST Foundation, San Francisco: 1977.

Pask, G., 'Consciousness'. *Proc. 4th European Meeting on Cybernetics and Systems Research*, Linz: Austria, 1978.

Pask, G. and B. C. E. Scott, 'Learning Strategies and Individual Competence'. *Int. J. Man-Machine Studies* 4, 217-253, 1972.

Pask, G. and B. C. E. Scott, 'CASTE: a system for exhibiting learning strategies and regulating uncertainty'. *Int. J. Man-Machine Studies* 5, 15-52, 1973.

Pask, G., B. C. E. Scott and D. Kallikourdis, 'A Theory of Conversations and Individuals' *Int. J. Man-Machine Studies* 5, 443-566, 1973.

Pask, G., D. Kallikourdis and B. C. E. Scott, 'The Representation of Knowables' *Int. J. Man-Machine Studies* 17, 15-134, 1975.

Petri, C. A., *Communications with Automata* (Clifford F. Green, Jr., trans.), A Supplement to Tech. Doc. Report for Rome Air Development Center, Contract No AF30(602)-3324, 1965.

Piaget, J., *Le Structuralisme* (Maschler, trans.) – 1971 – as *Structuralism*, London: Routledge and Kegan Paul, 1968.

Rapaport, R., *Pigs for the Ancestors*, Princeton: Princeton University Press, 1968.

Rapaport, A., 'Some Comments on 'Prisoner's Dilemma: Metagames and Other Solutions',' *Behavioral Science* 20, 3, 206-208, 1976.

Robinson, M., 'Prisoner's Dilemma, Metagames and other Solutions' *Behavioral Science* 20, 3, 201-206 (p. 209 as reply), 1976a.

Robinson, M., Human social groups: a cybernetic account of stability and instability (Ph.D. Thesis), Brunel University, 1976b.

Schon, D. A., *Displacement of Concepts*, London: Tavistock Publications, 1963.

Schumacher, E. F. *Small is Beautiful*, London: Blond and Briggs, 1973.

Schwartz, T., 'The Palian Movement in the Admiralty Islands'. *Anthropological Papers of American Museum of Natural History* 49, Part 2, 1962.

Tyler Bonner, J., *Cells and Societies*, Princeton, N. J.: Princeton University Press, 1958.

Toffler, A., *Future Shock*, New York: Random House, 1970.

Valosinov, V. N., *Freudianism. A Marxist Critique*, (trans. I. R. Thunik) N. H. Bruss (ed.), New York: Academic Press, 1976.

Varela, F., 'A calculus for self reference'. *Int. J. General Systems* 2, 5-24, 1975.

Varela, F. and J. Goguen, 'The Arithmetic of Closure' Proc. *3rd European Meeting on Cybernetics and Systems Research*, R. Trappl (ed.), Vienna; 1976.

Vickers, G., *Value Systems and Social Process*, Harmondsworth: Pelican Books, 1970.

Von Foerster, H., Various papers on microfiche, Biological Comp. Lab., University of Ill. Pub.: Illinois Blueprint Corp, 821 Bond, Peoria, Illinois 61603, 1976.

Vygotsky, L. S., *Thought and Language*, The M.I.T. Press, Cambridge, Mass.: 1962.

Wynne-Edwards, W. C., *Animal Dispersion*, London: Oliver and Boyd, 1963.

Waddington, C. H., *The Strategy of the Genes*, London: George Allen and Unwin, 1957.

Actors, games, and systems: the dialectics of social action and system structuring*

Tom Baumgartner, Tom R. Burns and Philippe DeVillé

1. Introduction

This paper outlines a systems theoretic approach with which to describe and analyze how, and under what conditons, processes and structures of social systems develop, stabilize, decay or undergo transformation. Our theoretical perspective draws on and attempts to develop modern systems theory (Ashby, 1957; Buckley, 1967, 1968; Deutsch, 1963; Katz and Kahn, 1966) and game theory (Luce and Raiffa, 1957; Rapoport, 1960; von Neumann and Morgenstern, 1953). The inspiration of Marxian theory and research is also apparent.

This first part outlines general ideas and assumptions underlying what is referred to as *actor-oriented systems analysis*.[1] This approach addresses itself to: (1) systems including social institutions as sources of constraint and regulation of social action and interaction – and, in particular, as determinants of the varying opportunities of different actors or classes of actors, and (2) actors and their activities as driving forces for the maintenance and change of system structures and processes, thereby shaping the conditions for social activity. In this sense, one may speak of the dialectical relationship between social action and systems. Section 2 suggests a few applications of such an approach. In Section 3, key conceptual elements are presented, and Section 4 summarizes methodological features and research guidelines of the approach.

1.1. Actors and systems

Two fundamentally different conceptions of human action underly most

* We are grateful to Walter Buckley and Eivind Jahren for their comments and suggestions on an earlier draft.

modeling of social behavior and social systems. In one, social actors are viewed as the essential force which structures and restructures social systems and the conditions of human activity; the individual, the historic personality, as exemplified by Schumpeter's entrepreneur, enjoys an extensive freedom to act within and upon social systems, and in this sense is independent of them. From the other viewpoint, social actors are reduced to faceless, rational automata following the iron rules of optimal choice theory in a world of constraints over which they lack control. This perspective excludes conflicting interests and values, divided loyalties, heterogeneous and incompatible goals, and true uncertainty (which is not the same as probabilistic uncertainty). Human action as a creative-destructive force is also absent.

To a large extent, social systems theories have been based on the second viewpoint,[2] reflecting an affinity to systems engineering and possibly the influence of what is considered the most advanced and successful social science, economics, which has assimilated most clearly the deterministic natural science paradigm. This type of approach tends to deny free decision and action space to human actors, since this leads to indeterminacies. Powerful and powerless actors, conflict and struggle, uneven developments and their possible reversals are also typically absent from consideration. System maintenance and reproduction, rather than being treated as problematical, are considered 'natural' and taken for granted in system modeling and analysis.[3] Purposeful action to assure system reproduction is not seen as necessary; struggles to transform social systems are given minimal attention.

In addition to addressing itself to system properties and dynamics, social systems modeling and analysis should, in our view, entail concepts and a methodology which enable specification of what actors, as purposeful, self-reflective beings, are all about, their decision-making and strategic capabilities, and their relation to system dynamics and stability. The systems framework outlined and illustrated briefly in this paper is partly inspired by such considerations.

As indicated earlier, actor-oriented systems analysis draws on game theory, which is grounded, of course, on concepts of actors, their interests, conflicts, decisions, and strategic actions in relation to one another. But in traditional game theory and its various off-shoots in the social sciences, games are conceptualized and analyzed as *closed systems*. This neglects an important feature of real-life 'games' or interaction situations, namely that game structure is to a large extent constructed (e.g. by the designer of game experiments) and that actors often can and do attempt to transform unsatisfactory game structures (Buckley et al., 1974).

Actor-oriented systems analysis, while trying to incorporate into a more global framework the valuable analytical approach provided by game theory, treats games as open, multi-level systems of social action. They change and develop. Game structuring and restructuring processes are identified as higher or meta-level operations maintaining or changing components of a game or system of social action. Our investigation of such *game transformation* processes has had two major concerns:

- to specify and analyze the material, social structural, and cultural constraints which structure conflict situations or game and conflict patterns and developments. At the same time social activities, partially determined by this context, constitute a fluid and dynamic force maintaining or changing it (in accordance with the premise of the human capability to structure and transform games).
- to ground game analysis in a theory of social action which, above all, stresses the transformational potentialities and tendencies of such action, in particular the capacity to structure and transform games.

In the first instance, attention is given to the ways in which specific aspects of the game context structure and restructure games: in particular, actors' definition of the social situation, their goals and preferences, available options, and interaction outcomes. In the second instance, one investigates the extent to which actors with different social relationships and cultural understandings not only respond and interact differently *in the context*, for example, of 'zero-sum', 'prisoners' dilemma', or other objective game conditions;[4] but also the extent to which they act differently *on the context*, structuring and transforming games. In this way, they may generate various development paths of games and game systems.

1.2. Actor-oriented systems analysis

This approach takes as its point of departure – and attempts to elucidate – the fundamental duality of the human situation: freedom and determinism. Human individuals and groups are subject to material, social structural and cultural constraints on their actions, yet they are at the same time creative, active forces who, in part, make their history. Social science research, in general, and social systems analysis in particular, should in our view try to avoid the danger of reifying institutions as well as assuming human powerlessness in the face of natural and environmental forces (which in any case are partly shaped by human activity). This leads to unjustifiably *underestimating* the capability of mankind to diminish or overcome material, social structural and cultural constraints through creative restructuring (Zeitlin, 1975:257). But, at the same time, one should not assume an *unrealistic power* of human actors to shape and transform their material, social structural, and cultural conditions, thereby ignoring or minimizing those constraining factors over which the degree of control is limited.

The focus on the interrelatedness of freedom and determinism of human action suggests the similarities and differences between Marxist analysis and our approach. Within the Marxist tradition, two different approaches to the problem of the reproduction and transformation of the capitalist system have been developed. The first, as exemplified by the structuralist formulation of Louis Althusser, is to a large extent a deterministic, 'causal-explanatory' approach. The fundamental structures of the capitalist system are the basis on which its morphostatic as well as morphogenetic nature are explained. The structural dominance of one class over the other reproduces itself through a wide spectrum of economic, ideological-cultural, political and social institutional mechanisms. But at the same time, the structural antagonisms between the classes – continuously generated by the contradictions between the relations and forces of production – are postulated to lead deterministically to a fundamental discontinuity in history, the revolution, destroying the self-reproducing nature of the system. In such a framework, human action as purposeful, self-reflective action is almost totally absent.

In contrast to such a structuralist Marxism, one can find also within the Marxist tradition a much more 'idealistic-voluntaristic' approach, for example in the works of George Lukács. Here the focus is on proletarian man, who through adequate *consciousness* of his own exploitation, assumes the revolutionary nature of his historical role – the abolishment of capitalism – and acts on this basis. The emphasis is on the inherent rationality of the proletarian man as 'universal man' who is able to transcend the structural contradictions of the capitalist system.

These two poles have yet to be systematically and effectively integrated within Marxist theory. One strategy with which to tackle this problem may be, as suggested here, to relate a systems approach – which can be found in Marxist theory – to a more developed *theory of social action*.

Our approach entails the development of methods, concepts, and models suitable for investigating, describing how, and under what conditions, processes and structures in social systems are formed, reproduced, and transformed. Particular attention is given to incompatibilities and conflicts in the systems, as well as to structure-changing or transformational tendencies. Moreover, human intentionality and social action are explicitly related to system stability and change. System stability, in particular, implies purposeful action to maintain the system, which, in the absence of such activity, would tend to change (De Villé and Burns, 1977). Such an approach goes beyond the more usual assumptions and features of modern systems and cybernetic modeling. In particular, while the latter give minimal attention to incompatibility and conflict in systems as well as to structure changing or transformational tendencies, these matters are central in actor-oriented systems analysis.

Research based on actor-oriented systems analysis has focused particularly on the following:

- System maintaining (reproduction) and system changing (transforming) processes, that is *structuring processes* and their relationship to what are referred to as 'process-level' conditions and activities (e.g. conflict and exchange activities).
- The capability of social actors to partially structure and restructure social systems and societal development, at the same time that the latter constrain interaction possibilities and influence the structure of power in society. The dual nature of social action – that is, as system maintaining and system changing forces – is particularly stressed. (This duality is often revealed through contradictions among processes and through conflicts between and among actors).
- The simultaneous conflict and harmony of interests among actors in a social system, particularly as these relate to the maintenance and transformation of social system structures and processes.

2. Structuring of social systems

A social system consists of interdependent spheres of social action, e.g. political and economic spheres or sub-systems.[5] System components are linked to one another in the susual causal relationships and feedback loops as well as through structuring processes and linkages. *Structuring* is an operator on processes, functions and relationships generally, rather than on variables (Baumgartner et al., 1977a, 1976a). In this sense, structuring represents a higher order form of determination or causality.

Structuring or 'structure-level' factors shape and regulate 'process-level' conditions, processes, and activities, e.g. shaping the opportunities and constraints, incentives and meanings within which social activity – production, exchange, influence, and conflict as understood in traditional interaction analysis – takes place.[6] Our approach entails specifying the higher order structuring processes and variables (e.g. specific morphostatic and morphogenic processes) and their relation to lower level relationships and processes in a social system; the maintenance and transformation of the latter are analyzed in terms of the operation of such structuring factors. In other words, we try to formulate a *multi-level model* of social system stability and change, which accounts for particular system structures and processes in different contexts or in different time periods (that is, situationally specific invariances) and variation in system structure and processes from one context to another or from one time period to another.

The characteristic processes and structures of a social system are the result of multiple, often inconsistent structuring factors – such factors provide a *context* for any given social system. A major factor in such structuring is human action itself; that is, humans through their activities, intentionally and unintentionally, structure and restructure social systems, in particular, their characteristic processes and structures. Key structuring factors examined in our research are the following, among others:

– deliberate human action and planning, the exercise of 'meta-power' and relational control by social actors;
– cultural and ideational factors;
– structuring processes as unintended or secondary consequences of social action;
– technology and material conditions;
– uncontrolled or uncontrollable factors operating as structuring 'forces'.

Below, several instances of our investigation and analysis of structuring and restructuring in social life are discussed briefly to suggest the concrete applicability of the approach as well as to point at properties of social relations and processes which are structured. Structuring through the manipulation of management of systems of social action is particularly stressed.

2.1. Structuring of conflict and cooperation

Here we have tried to provide a means with which to describe and analyze the dynamics and complexity of social conflict: the possible involvement of multiple actors (with varying perspectives and interests) at different levels and in different spheres of social action, the formation of new collective actors, and the fragmentation or collapse of others. Above all, we have been concerned with the structuring and development aspects of most social conflicts (Baumgartner et al., 1975b, 1977b, 1978c).

In general, the form, course, and outcome of conflict processes – for instance, relating to conflict settlement or conflict development – depend on contextual factors such as the following (Baumgartner et al., 1978c; Coleman, 1957; Deutsch, 1973; Kriesberg, 1973; Simmel, 1964):

- the type of social relations the actors have or develop, in particular, the extent to which they have solidary relations, the number and strength of cooperative linkages, etc.;
- the normative and value context to a conflict, specifically the extent to which the actors share a common vision or image of the appropriate institutional framework or rules within which conflicts are to be settled;
- the social matrix in which the actors' social relations are imbedded, for instance, cross-cutting identifications, common allegiances and memberships, and above all, the likelihood of effective third party intervention and structuring of the conflict process.

Established social relationships are a major factor structuring conditions and activities on the process-level. Consider a situation, for instance, involving management and labor in the context of a production setting where their interests and goals are in conflict and where no outcome acceptable to both sides appears feasible *within* the existing set of options, rules of the game, and other institutional conditions. Typically, in such a case actors explore, individually or collectively, possibilities of trying to generate new options, change game rules, or restructure institutional features. At least two families of transformation patterns may be distinguished. On the one hand, if the relationships between the actors are antagonistic, they will be predisposed to oppose one another in transforming a game, each trying to increase his or her chances of gaining (or avoiding losses) at the expense of others in the situation. Mutually satisfying conflict settlements will be unlikely in such cases. This contributes to reproduction of the antagonistic social relations. On the other hand, if the actors have solidary social relations, the likelihood is increased that they will cooperate in transforming conflict situations so as to obtain mutually satisfactory outcomes. In other words, actors with solidary social relations have a capability and predispositon – within certain limits, of course – to transform conflict situations so as to settle conflicts in mutually satisfying ways, and, hence, to reinforce and reproduce their solidary relationships.

Although social relationships play a major role in the structuring and restructuring of social interaction conditions and processes, there are additional (but related) factors such as the normative and value context. The more actors share a common set of concepts and norms *guiding the structuring and restructuring of institutional arrangements,* the more likely they can agree to an institutional change (including institutional innovations) to settle a conflict which does not appear resolvable within the existing institutional set-up. In general, actors' images of appropriate or effective institutional arrangements and solutions to a conflict have a substantial impact on the course of a conflict.

Third parties (making up the context of a two-actor conflict process) may intervene to transform or to facilitate transforming game conditions and rules so as to either develop or resolve conflict. The conflict settlement role is frequently institutionalized as in many industrial and industrializing societies where the state intervenes in and regulates capital/labor interactions and disputes (and also other potentially conflicting relationships) through the use of legislation, mediation, arbitration as well as other strategies,[7] (e.g. see our analysis of the Lip factory conflict (Baumgartner et al., 1978c) which points up the effect of a specific social structural context (the government, judicial system, powerful industrial interests, and national labor unions) on the course and outcome of an escalating management/labor conflict (Baumgartner et al., 1975c).

2.2. Structuring of power systems

Actor-oriented systems analysis has been applied to the study of the structuring and restructuring of power structures and systems of stratification (e.g., Alker et al., 1978; Baumgartner et al., 1978a, 1978b; Burns, 1976). This approach to the study of social power entails investigation and analysis of *structuring processes which have led historically to the emergence and development (or failure to develop as well as collapse) of social control hierarchies and more systemic forms of power*. The research focuses on (1) positive feedback loops, linking initial power differences to differential accumulation of power resources among actors or categories of actors and (2) on contexts for such feedback loops to occur, for example either situations where opportunities for subordinate actors and groups to withdraw or emigrate are minimal, or where possibilities for subordinate actors to communicate, organize and to act collectively to constrain accumulation processes are absent or problematical. Under such conditions, resource accumulation and power development are likely to occur. Initial differences, even quite small ones, in positional advantage and resource control may be amplified into major institutional advantage and resource control may be amplified into major institutionalized class structures. These developments, combined with *inter*-societal exchange, competition, and conflict, tend to reinforce internal social stratification as well as stratification among societies. Such processes have been examined in our research in relation to the emergence and development of the state, empire, and other social formations (Baumgartner et al., 1976b).

A basic principle underlying our approach is that initial social differentiation among actors in a social system in terms of resource control and action capability typically contributes to *differential accumulation of resources* through processes of social interaction (e.g. exchange, conflict, and influence processes).[8] Often, this can be translated into *structuring or meta-power*, that is the power to change the rules of the game, the matrix of action and interaction possibilities and their outcomes, and social orientations in the context of which social action takes place. This offers further opportunities to gain control over resources (additional accumulation) and to maintain as well as to develop social power differences. The overall process entails the differential accumulation and uneven development of action capabilities and resource control among actors; it may take the following characteristic form, among others:

1. Initial differences in action possibilities or in resource control among actors leads to unequal payoffs through conflict, exchange, and influence processes (or social interaction generally).[9] The unequal payoffs make for future differentials in the action capabilities and resource control among the actors, both within the system to which they belong as well as with respect to other systems (and their actors). This is particularly the case where there is little or no institutional or normative regulation to prevent or limit such amplification (see Note 8).
2. These differences in action capabilities and resource control translate into differential probabilities for further accumulation. For instance, advantaged actors to a greater extent than others are enabled to generate

or to exploit new action or exchange opportunities, to prevent or control negative consequences or developments, or to structure themselves and their environments to their advantage. Above all, those who are advantaged in action capabilities and resource control often have greater opportunities to produce, maintain, or change social networks and structures and, in general, to restructure social institutions to a greater or lesser extent to their own benefit. Thus, they may be enabled to transgress or overcome institutionalized and normative constraints on power accumulation.

By using their power to define the rules of the game and to shape the matrix of action possibilities and payoffs, they can attract supporters and weaken opponents. Supporters and dependents, in turn, can be used to engage on yet a larger scale in exercising structuring power and relational control. Ultimately, an elite or power group *A* in such a position may be able to construct and maintain under its control a system of hierarchical control structures and networks with loyal or compliant supporters or participants. At the same time, *A* and his agents may, through divide and rule strategies, erode or weaken competing or opposing segments of society and the structures and processes which they control. In this way, conditions and processes which might countervail and restrict *A*'s power and power development are socially impeded or regulated.

3. As a result of processes such as those described in (1) and (2) an amplification of power differences proceeds whereby an elite or power group *A* gains advantages in systemic power relative to competing or potentially competing groups. A highly differentiated social structure and network system under *A*'s hegemony emerges and develops. This may be used to carry out *A*'s will or policies with respect to the larger society and to control or limit the action possibilities of opponents or potential opponents.

Such a positive feedback loop between initial power differences and differential accumulation of resources and societal power occurs in different social structural, material, and cultural contexts (Baumgartner et al., 1976b). Below, we try to specify a few of the settings or contexts in which power and resource accumulation processes are likely to emerge and continue.

a. Those with initial power advantage attract followers and additional resources away from those with less advantage, and they use these to reformulate and restructure rules, institutional arrangements, and social relations, in such a way as to amplify their power advantages and resource control possibilities.[10] Of course, *a major consideration here is the extent to which there are increasing surplus resources available, for example, by virtue of the expansion of production (through new technology, increases in the labor force or in other factors of production), territorial conquest, trade expansion, new bases for legitimizing taxation, etc.*

b. Ownership and inheritance rules and rights (as opposed to norms of redistribution and corrective institutional devices to limit or prevent accumulation processes) sustain and legitimize differential accumulation of resources. A power group or elite *A* often uses an initial power advantage – through processes such as those referred to in (a) – to strengthen ownership and inheritance concepts and practices. These in turn stabilize and even accelerate accumulation processes, thus contributing to the reproduction and elaboration of the stratification system benefiting *A*.

c. Weaker actors lack group consciousness and organization or control over important resources. Thus, they are not in a position to oppose the accumulation processes or the restructuring of social conditions by the power group or elite *A*. Processes and conditions tending to fragment or weaken opposition groups which previously have played a critical role in limiting *A*'s power are especially important in permitting a process of power accumulation to continue or even to accelerate. Of course, powerful actors may initiate or maintain such conditions of fragmentation through divide and rule strategies (see Note 7).

d. Demographic movements across societal boundaries often serve to amplify the power of *A*. On the one hand, the import of persons or groups who are or become dependent on *A* can contribute to *A*'s power to organize collective action wthin the society. On the other hand, *A*'s power position is improved and stabilized by the emigration or exile of opposition persons and groups who countervail or restrict *A*'s power and its development.[11] Such emigration opens up opportunities for the selective recruitment and promotion of loyal persons and groups into political and economic roles vacated by emigrants – manipulations which serve the purpose of gaining and stabilizing commitment to the existing regime (Hardin, 1976). That is, there is a direct relationship between emigration possibilities and the development and stabilization of hierarchical structures, provided the resultant loss of population does not undermine significantly the economic base of the society, yet effectively removes those who strongly oppose the established social order (and whose opposition would tend to weaken it).[12]

e. In a wide range of contexts the development and maintenance of social hierarchy is facilitated by constraints on the emigration (or withdrawal) possibilities of subordinate individuals and groups, under the specific conditions where their productive capabilities and resources (labor, the products of labor, other resources) are not replaceable. For instance, historically, the emergence and development of classical state and empire formations have been associated with a dense growing population practicing agriculture in a fertile region which is circumscribed geographically or socially (Caneiro, 1970; Baumgartner et al., 1976b). The constraints on the emigration possibilities of those who have been subordinated through military, economic or other means enabled their labor and the products of their labor to be mobilized and appropriated by those in superior positions. Such constraint may arise from physical or social environments. For example, an ecological setting of fertile lands suitable for farming surrounded by infertile, arid, or mountainous areas constrains farming populations, at least in early history, from leaving the area. Or the constraints may be social structural in nature: Members of a community are prevented from moving to neighboring areas or alternative territorial systems by the presence of other ethnic, religious, national or cultural groups capable of blocking passage; or there are powerful incentives to stay close to allies or potential allies for protection in case of attack. Or the area, relative to its surrounding areas, is highly developed or abundant with resources, economically tying persons or groups to the locale (that is, the opportunity costs of migrating are especially high). Or religious beliefs tie them to the area.

Historically, the establishment of national frontiers has been a major instrument of structuralization (Finer, 1975; Baumgartner et al., 1976b, 1975d; Schumacher, 1973). Societal boundary control to prevent or inhibit migratory movements is established using the administrative and police powers of a more or less well-developed state. This may also entail limitations on internal movement.[13]

If subordinate actors are able to exit – to use the metaphor of Hirschman (1970) – then an elite is limited to manipulating payoff structures and making normative appeals in order to establish and maintain hierarchical structures and to accomplish its ends. Of course, hierarchical control structures may be built up using available resources to determine payoffs and, by this means, to structure social relationships and networks. But power based on the manipulation of payoffs does not usually provide opportunities to establish *absolute* domination.

If in a particular social context *A* has access to valuable resources which others do not have access to, at least not to the same degree, e.g. trade, slaves, land, and money, then *A* can establish social relationships in which subordinate actors are to some extent dependent on those resources. Such power is dependent, of course, upon the availability and continuity of control over resource flows and distribution by *A* and others committed to the institutionalized social hierarchy. But as long as there are alternative sources of the resources ultimately available – frontier land or other social systems or collectivities to migrate to or to participate in, then it is impossible for *A* to *absolutize* the relationships, since the use of the resources is still limited to the manipulation of payoffs.[14] For subordinate actors in this case, submission to *A*'s power is marginally better than attempting to obtain the necessary goods from another source. An element of choice is still involved: If *A* pushes *B* (or the *B*'s) too far, the latter simply leave. Hence, hierarchical structure will tend to be limited in degree of stability.

This suggests that differential control over resources, in and of itself, is not a sufficient condition to create lasting power structures. In the absence of real scarcity, it is difficult, if not impossible, to structure systems of extreme social domination or hierarchy in any permanent way by means of using resources-for-inducement. An absolute abundance of resources makes long-term subjugation and obvious, extreme exploitation most difficult to achieve and maintain.

To the extent that *A*'s resource accumulation and power development depends on the production of resources by *B* which *A* then appropriates – for example through unequal exchange – then opportunities for *B*'s to emigrate or in general to withdraw effectively limit accumulation and stratification *to a level which B finds acceptable or tolerates*. One may argue that, *in general, the more readily subordinate actors have access to basic resources outside of an A/B superordinate-subordinate system of relationships, the less A will be able to dominate B, exploit his labor or the products of his labor, and develop hierarchical control structures.* And if extreme subordination does develop, *the system is unlikely to remain stable, specifically under conditions where the emigrating subordinates (or their products) are not readily replaceable* (see Note 14).[15]

In sum, geographical and technological conditions as well as those of a social structural and ideological character contribute to shaping the formation and development of social structure. In our framework, this is seen to take place by their facilitating or constraining action opportunities and influencing payoffs – particularly in a manner so as to differentiate groups in society. Again, it should be stressed that elites and power groups themselves try to manipulate social action and interaction conditions in order to structure social relationships, processes, and their behavioral consequences in a manner favorable to themselves. The evolution of higher level social control strategies, techniques, and institutions has occurred through individuals and groups discovering for themselves various methods of control as well as adopting methods discovered by others. Of particular interest in this regard has been the development of more sophisticated strategies for planning, meta-management, and integration of multiple social structures and networks.

3. Conceptual and methodological features

The point of departure of the actor-oriented systems approach consist of several general theoretical and methodological premises, which are considered basic to any attempt at model building and analysis in the social sciences. Although the discussion which follows is abstract, the concepts and principles suggest specific guidelines in the construction of models of social structures and processes.

3.1. Systems of social action

Social action systems (production in the broadest sense) consist of patterned social action and interaction, which are shaped and influenced by – at the same time that they produce, reproduce, and transform – material, social structural, and cultural constraints. Such systems are characterized by the following components:
- a set of actors
- activity, problem or issue area(s) with respect to which the actors have certain interests and goals (not necessarily compatible).
- rules, norms, guiding concepts and assumptions ('the rules of the game') defining the situation, the type of game the actors are to play, etc.
- interests and goals of the actors in relation to one another in the context of the activity area, their evaluative bases, and perceptual models in the situation.
- the distribution of action and interaction possibilities (including resource control) among different actors or categories of actors.

– the likely outcomes, or costs and benefits (including spin-off and spill-over effects) of actions and interactions for different actors or categories of actors.

3.2. Interrelatedness of things

Social life is characterized by its complex interrelatedness. A social system consists of interdependent spheres of social action and subsystems which are, however, partially autonomous with respect to one another. That is, they are differentiated from one another at the same time that linkages – traditional causal relationships and feedback loops, as well as, and more importantly, direct and indirect multi-stranded and multi-level relationships – are found among them (see Note 16). Such systems possess properties and modes of action distinct from those of the constituent elements. In a word, there are interaction and aggregation effects which frequently cannot be derived from the properties of the elements.

Social processes, actions and interactions have multiple and varied ramifications, because actors and resources are constituent elements of two or more spheres of social action (e.g. economic, political, social, and cultural sub-systems). Thus, social processes of production and distribution generate multiple effects, spin-offs and spill-overs, in the sphere of production and distribution itself as well as in other spheres of social life. This is the basis of the multi-stranded linkages among spheres and sub-systems and of the unintended consequences of purposeful human action.[16]

3.3. Control, power, and meta-power

Property rights, and control rights more generally, and the different positions and roles of actors (or classes of actors) in social systems give them qualitatively and quantitatively different relationships to the socially valued products (including their spin-offs and spill-overs) of social activity. These valuables include not only material goods and resources, but also labor power, knowledge and capabilities, social characteristics such as status, authority and charisma, and positions in social structures linking actors to particular valuables and other actors.

Control over valuables provides controlling actors with power and meta-power. Power is the ability of actors to bring about or influence social actions and outcomes favorable to their interests *within* an institutionalized social action context. Meta-power or structuring power is the ability to influence and structure (again, within the limits of a yet higher-order context) an institutionalized framework of social action. The exercise of meta-power entails the manipulation or change of rules of the game, distribution of resources and action possibilities, interaction outcomes, and cultural orientations – in general, the conditions of social action in a particular system. Clearly, although an actor may have power within an interaction setting or game, he or she may or may not have the meta-power to manipulate and change the action setting, the constraints which institutionally define the power of actors' exercise of behavioral control with respect to one another.[17]

3.4. Differential accumulation and uneven development

Access to and exercise of control over societal valuables varies among classes of actors (e.g. capitalists vs. workers) as well as among actors of a given category (e.g. skilled vs. unskilled workers). This variation in control over valuables and the various spin-offs and spill-overs of productive and exchange activities leads to differential accumulation of resources, capabilities, and valuables in general. In other words, distribution among societal actors of costs and benefits of production and exchange is unequal (see Note 8).

Differential accumulation among actors translates into uneven formation of development capabilities – the ability of actors or classes of actors to shape or take advantage of action opportunities, to avoid undesirable effects, or to structure and restructure the conditions of social action and interaction to their own advantage. In a word, differences in power and meta-power are generated.

Changes in the distrubution of access to and control over societal valuables, and ultimately changes in meta-power to determine the context and rules of social action, may favor those who have a different vision or model of appropriate or effective institutions. As a result, new institutions are established, typically with different power and meta-power implications than those of the previous social system. In this way system development depends on resource distribution, e.g. the distribution resulting from institutionalized as well as emergent system processes.

3.5. Structuring of systems

As suggested earlier, social systems consist of interdependent spheres of action which are partially autonomous as well as open. System openness and complexity as well as power struggles generate 'localized' changes in economic, political, socio-cultural and other spheres of social action, which are incompatible with one another and with the existing system as a whole. That is, the multiple spheres are incompatible to a greater or lesser extent in their relationships (and operations) to one another as well as in relation to overall properties, processes and relationships which give a system its identity. A social system is therefore not assumed to be necessarily well-integrated and self-regulating. Rather, societal processes and forces within and between spheres may often operate in opposition to one another. Attainment of stability in one sub-system may produce instability in other sub-systems. Achievement of a goal or objective in one part can mean failure to achieve goals or objectives in other parts. Thus, the system *as a whole*, viewed as a complex, dynamic totality, is rarely, if at all, in equilibrium. System stability must be explained in the face of ever-present tendencies for structures to reform, change, or evolve. The stress is therefore on the morphogenic potentialities and tendencies of social systems in a dynamic world of change and flux.

Structuring factors, whether arising from a social system's environment, system-environment dynamics, or internal dynamics of the system, (1) affect directly or indirectly *multiple* factors, components or sub-sytems of the social system; (2) affect multiple components or subsystems *differentially*; and (3) often affect them in *incompatible or contradictory ways*. Structuring processes and forces may restructure or transform some processes and structures in a system at different rates, with differential irreversibility, or more strongly or in qualitatively different ways than others. That is, multiple effects are produced and some of these work at cross-purposes or in opposition to one another, for instance, tending both to maintain and to change system properties. In such ways, changes in material, social-structural, cultural or social features of a social system frequently produce divergent developments.

The multiple, often inconsistent structuring processes and conditions are a major part of the 'historical forces' underlying the institutions of society at a given time, as well as of the dynamics of new institutional forms continually struggling to emerge.

Dialectical processes in social systems entail, generally speaking, contradictory or conflicting social processes as well as dialogue-like competing 'social forces'.[18] Contradictory processes entail two or more processes or structuring factors which come into relation to one another and work inconsistently or at cross-purposes. It is possible for the same process to do this by generating multiple effects, some of which work in opposition to one another. The role of human cognition and reflection in social processes also suggests that 'contradictions' be interpreted literally to include as well oppositions in symbolically communicated principles of social organization.

3.6. Social reproduction and transformation

Social systems are products of human action, that is, they are artificial, and subject to continual morphogenic pressures. Maintenance of system stability therefore requires continual reproductive and structuring activitties in response to system contradictions, patterns of conflict, and changes in system environments.[19] We speak of *social reproduction* when stability or continuity of characteristic social structures and processen occurs. This entails not only their maintenance during a given time period but the production or acquisition of necessary and possibly sufficient resources for their perpetuation in subsequent time periods. Thus, social reproduction depends on replacing the instruments or other means of activity (production) as well as on the maintenance and replacement of actors (reproduction of labor power). It also entails structuring the context of social activity, e.g. in the case of economic production, the structuring of the political and socio-cultural spheres.[20]

Social reproduction depends on three factors (Burns, 1976):

- possession, on the part of actors engaged in structuring activity, of a model of society to guide activities reproducing a particular social structure, process, or other feature;
- interest and commitment on their part to mobilize and utilize resources in the reproduction process;
- sufficient resources, capabilities, and power and meta-power to carry out effective reproduction.

The meta-power capability of actors to initiate and control processes of producing and reproducing institutional arrangements has, of course, to be itself reproduced, and, in a changing environment, typically requires adapting models, interests and resource capabilities. Even so, power and meta-power redistributions, continuous environmental interference, and a contradictory integration of sub-systems may make reproduction impossible.

An institutional arrangement not only generates particular intended outcomes. There are also various spin-offs and spill-overs, which operate to *reproduce* the arrangement, as well as effects operating to undermine or *transform* the arrangement. Often these are unintended consequences of the policies and actions of dominant groups. Such 'contradictions' may emerge because: (1) The model utilized by the actors fails to specify and does not enable evaluation of conditions and processes which erode the system; e.g. new possibilities of social action or new types of outcome emerge which provide powerful incentives for patterns of social action *incompatible* with the existing institutional set-up. Actors participating in the setting may even unwittingly produce the transformed situation as an unintended consequence of their own policies and activities. (2) Incentives may be such as to tempt actors into the pursuit of interests or activities incompatible with the maintenance and reproduction of the system. Frequently, actors become engaged – for instance, for economic or political reasons – in other institutional areas and social relationships which make competing or greater claims on their loyalties and interests. This then weakens or erodes their commitment to or interest in social reproduction of a particular institutional set-up. (3) Finally, the actors may lack the action capability or power to carry out effective structuring activities in the face of restructuring forces or action on the part of others. In particular, when shifts in power favor those with a different model or blueprint of the system, and those actors perceive a net gain in bringing about a change, then restructuring is likely to occur. This will take place, of course, against the will of those committed to the previous institutional set-up.[21]

Institutionalized social relationships and social relational ideology – on the basis of which actors expect certain patterns of behavior from one another and are disposed to interact in patterned ways – shape *concrete interaction settings* among actors: they do this by structuring action opportunities, payoffs, and social orientations of the actors to one another. But at the same time, the social relationships and ideology may be contradicted or incompatible with the very interactions they contribute to producing in the concrete action settings. Such contradictions occur because the established or institutionalized social relationships and relational ideology *only partially determine* the conditions of action and interaction actually occurring. Other social factors as well as material conditions (geographical, climactical, technological, and other aspects of the physical environment) – *outside of the domain or control inherent in the social relationships and relational ideology* – structure and influence action and interaction patterns. In particular, since relational ideology can never completely model or represent all relevant or significant factors, above all those which emerge as new elements in the situation, there are unanticipated events and unintended consequences of the actions and interactions of the actors themselves. Such contradictions frequently lead to socio-cultural restructuring: new social relationships and ideologies may emerge which are more compatible with actual interaction conditions (Burns, 1976).[22]

The relationships between human actors (or producers) and the social and cultural worlds, their products, is a dialectical one. Human institutions, which may appear 'objective and overwhelming' are a humanly produced or constructed objectivity (Godelier, 1973). Rules and institutional arrangements are more or less open to frequent re-interpretation, reappraisal and re-construction for practical purposes in the cause of action and the performance of tasks. But at the same time, rules and institutional arrangements act to structure interaction patterns, social relationships, and culture. To the degree that they shape action possibilities and consequences, often in unintended ways, they become an impersonal power – much like the natural environment – although they have been created and are maintained through human activities.

3.7. Conflict and social transformation

As already suggested, social systems cannot be assumed to be well integrated and automatically self-regulating. Divergent developments will occur and conflicting social forces will operate in any social system. Different social actors and classes are likely to be associated in differing degrees and in qualitatively different ways to the discordant developments (see Sections 3.3 and 3.4 above). Those adversely affected by the operation or development of the institutional set-up may be able to socially articulate their disadvantage and deprivation, e.g. in terms of norms and values about fairness or equity (or orther ideological grounds). They may also be organized – or able to organize, particularly in democratic societies – and mobilize to carry out social actions to change the institutional set-up or at least its undesirable features (from their viewpoint). These activities usually bring them into conflict with those having an interest or commitment to system reproduction. That is, conflict arises concerning the maintenance (or reproduction) as opposed to the restructuring and possible transformation of the institutional set-up. Such conflict can interfere with or obstruct reproduction processes, setting the stage for social transformation.

Much of our current research is focused on the *continuous process of system structuring and restructuring*, that is, on the multiple, often inconsistent, processes which operate to produce and transform social formations (particular systems of power, conflict, and exchange). Subsumed by the notion of contradictory structuring processes is the concept of social conflict and struggle among groups engaged in these processes, above all, conflict processes with respect to maintaining, reproducing, or transforming social structures and processes in a society.

4. Contextual analysis and multi-level modeling

The language and methodological approach developed and utilized in our work is oriented to the description and analysis of system stability and change. Two general principles underlie the approach:[23]

1. In social life, the existence of space and time invariances or lawful connections cannot be taken for granted (Herbst, 1971; Baumgartner et al., 1977a). Human systems are typically self-transforming systems (as opposed to mechanical systems) with morphogenic (or structure changing) potentialities and tendencies.
2. Changes in social system processes and structures can best be conceptualized, modeled, and analyzed from a multi-level perspective.

As suggested earlier, a social process often takes the specific form it does because of its context, and it may undergo transformations as a result of changes in context. Of particular interest are rules and patterns of social action and interaction which are dependent on specific settings. Ultimately, one seeks to specify and analyze factors bringing about changes in context: the social process itself may be such a factor. Such a contextual approach to the study of social phenomena calls for the development of models and tools which enable the modeling of the specific ways in which contexts structure or operate on the phenomena. For this purpose we utilize multi-level concepts and models.

A multi-level system or process is composed of sub-systems, one or more of which stand in qualitatively asymmetric or subordinate relationship to a dominant variable, process or sub-system. The latter regulates, operates upon, or changes the relationships of processen at the lower level, for example changing the parameters or coefficients of such relationships, or the relationships themselves. The morphogenic (structure changing) or morphostatic (structure preserving) tendencies of social systems are conceptualized in terms of the outputs of higher or *meta-level* processes or sub-systems structuring the processes, relationships, and parameters of lower level sub-systems. The meta-level processes may actually depend on or be influenced either by system inputs or outputs or developments inherent to the system, that is by lower-level events or processes.

In multi-level description and modeling, one attempts to represent and explain the particular structure of relationships between or among factors, structures of systems in a given context or historical period, and changes in that structure from one context to another and from one time period to another. On the basis of such an approach, one is interested not only in stating and utilizing 'causal' propositions such as 'when X, then Y', but in stating and utilizing propositions such as the following: 'because of the operation of a structuring or regulatory system, process, or variable Z – which may itself depend on processes within the system or the outputs of the system itself – the relationship X/Y can be expected to be maintained or to be changed significantly in such and such a way or to vanish altogether'.

We have suggested a fairly general and systematic framework for organizing and understanding better social processes and events, e.g. relating to conflict and power. Our particular action-oriented systems analysis is offered as an apparently useful beginning; it appears to organize a large mass of often unrelated data, and is compatible with the more dynamic and structural theories of social science. Some readers may prefer a large and more refined set of system components, and we hope that they may be inspired to develop them and carry the present, obviously limited effort further.

Notes

1. A number of published papers developing and applying various concepts of actor-oriented systems analysis are listed in the references under Alker, Baumgartner, Buckley, Burns, De Villé and Meeker.
2. Important exceptions to the general pattern are found in the works of Buckley (1967) and Geyer (1974, 1976).
3. This type of approach tends to separate system processes and structures. Although consideration may be given to how environment (and structure) determine processes, the processes and their outputs in turn are rarely seen to affect or transform the structures through dynamic feedback and feed-control linkages. This is the case, for example, with

economic growth models whose mathematical structure remains unaffected by model output. Similarly, macro-economic models have to be frequently re-estimated, particularly during periods of actual structural transformations, so that newer data 'bends' coefficients, at least somewhat, in the right direction (Baumgartner et al., 1977a, 1976a).

4. Objective game situations are defined by the rules of the game, e.g. rules concerning communication and the making of binding agreements, by the action and interaction possibilities, and their outcomes.
5. The abstract concept of a system is defined as a set of elements or components together with the set of relationships and processes connecting the elements. The network of linkages between elements is the organization of the system.
6. Of course, structure-level processes may themselves be structured by higher-level processes. In general, factors, relationships among variables, and processes in a social system depend on the context in which they occur. (See Sections 3 and 4).
7. Third party intervention aimed at maintaining or developing competitive or conflict processes is observable in 'divide and rule' strategies such as used by governments in anti-cartel regulation of markets. This entails determining the 'rules of the game'; structuring the aggregate action and interaction possibilities of those involved in the situation, for instance limiting their opportunities to associate or communicate; structuring the gains and losses associated with particular interactions in order to promote conflict or competiton, as in the creation of payoff structures such as 'zero-sum' or 'prisoners' dilemma'; or it can entail promoting distrust among the actors or an individualistic self-interest ideology (Burns and Buckley, 1974; Buckley et al., 1974).

   This study of the social structuring of conflict relationships has entailed, above all, investigation of the use of divide and rule strategies of differing degrees of sophistication in several social contexts. Although many historical and contemporary processes can be examined in such terms, slave, factory, and imperialist systems have provided particularly fruitful areas for this type of investigation (Baumgartner et al., 1975b; 1977d). We have also tried to explore how accidental or historically derived social fragmentations, much like manipulated ones, may contribute to the maintenance of a system of domination.
8. In the context of this type of analysis we have explored the relationship between social structure – and unequal control over strategic resources – and social exchange. A core idea is that exchange activity typically reinforces different internal structures and processes among interacting sub-systems or actors.
   1. Actors engaged in exchange are typically not equal in terms of their control over strategic resources, structural positions, and action capabilities. For instance, the distribution of property rights among them assigns control possibilities to varying degrees and extent over the disposition and use of resources.
   2. The differential powers of the actors engaged in exchange permit some more than others to generate or to take advantage of *new* action or exchange opportunities, to prevent or control negative consequences or vicious circles, and to structure themselves and their environments to their advantage. In the latter case, the more powerful actors are enabled to a greater or lesser extent to structure and restructure the conditions and rules of exchange activity, in this way often guaranteeing terms of exchange more favorable to themselves than others. Baumgartner and Burns (1975) and Baumgartner et al. (1976c) have analyzed three cases of such deliberate social structuring: the exchange relationship established between England and Portugal in the 17th Century, the structuring of Bretton Woods economic institutions, and the current struggle over the structuring of economic relationships between developed and less developed countries.
   3. Differences in action capabilities and power dependency positions among actors engaged in exchange lead to *structurally unequal exchange and uneven development patterns*. Among other things, these outcomes tend to reproduce the unequal power structure which has given rise to unequal exchange in the first place. In general, unequal

exchange and uneven development are likely to occur in interaction systems in which the distribution of power is unequal, unless the less powerful are substantially protected through social and political institutions.

The concepts of unequal exchange and uneven development are general ones and have been applied in the study of exchange activity at different societal levels (Burns, 1977): husband/wife exchange in family systems, employer/employee exchange in capitalist societies, and international economic exchange between developed and less developed countries.

9. Clearly, the conditions and processes which *maintain* and *elaborate* social differences may differ from those which *initiate* the process. Thus, social differentiation in control over resources or resource accumulation may arise because of the distributional rules associated with exchange or warfare. The resulting accumulation of resources by A may make possible yet further elaboration of the unequal relationships as well as the subordination of others, previously independent of, or co-equal with, A.
10. For example, a common pattern in the historical emergence of the state is the availability and acquisition by the central leadership of surplus resources which can be used for purposes of societal structuring. Typically, the center is enabled to attract and support a body of followers and dependents, using resources gained through warfare, trade and other economic activity, political alliance as well as various legitimation devices. The followers and dependents are the 'Lord's' or the 'King's men' supporting him and executing his will. Through them he gains the possibility of extending his capability to obtain additional resources (through taxation, tribute, territorial conquest, etc.) and to carry out structuring activities – to develop and maintain a hierarchical control structure under his hegemony even over the opposition of rivals and recalcitrant subordinates.
11. For example, the export of warriors such as in the early Norman states (12th and 13th centuries) may have contributed to stable internal structure. Also, emigration to the U.S. probably reduced internal turbulence in 19th century Europe and facilitated the trend to stable 'representative democracies'.
12. However, emigration or exile, which serves political purposes, can have a detrimental economic impact with possible long-term political ramifications. For instance, those who emigrate or are exiled are persons and groups with valuable skills and knowledge. Also, the emigrant population may be made up of persons or groups who would support and reinforce the regime and, therefore, this movement operates to undermine the existing socio-political structure. Pressure to emigrate often arises because of economic hardship or social conflict, e.g. ethnic conflicts, but nevertheless the structural and political effects may be those suggested above.
13. Of course, groups within the society may oppose the socially imposed constraints on the freedom of movement of particular groups or persons, since such conditions affect the distribution of power in society, strengthening stratification in some domains and possibly weakening it in others.

    Resources are required to carry out such 'boundary control' and hence represent costs not borne by societies which have naturally occurring environmental constraints or social constraints arising exogenously (hostile or alien neighbors). These differences often have long-term economic and political implications.
14. The unavailability of alternative sources is equivalent to monopoly over the distribution of resources. This constrains the action possibilities of those lacking such resource control; in other words, they lack the alternative of going outside the system to realize their goals or needs. Of course, dominant actors also try to make subordinates *believe* that there is no viable alternative source of the necessary resources, that is, that they in fact hold a monopoly.
15. Of course, there are degrees of replaceability. Also, in a more complete discussion, one would have to take up demographic factors generally, the role of population growth or

decline, changes in population structure, shifts in production freeing labor previously bound up, for instance in agricultural production, influx of women into the labor force, etc.

16. Sub-systems and spheres of social action in a social system are partially autonomous with respect to one another. That is, they are differentiated from one another at the same time that linkages and interactions, particularly structuring linkages, are found among them. In this way, they provide context for one another. Therefore, changes in one or more sub-systems – changes which may occur because of the partial autonomy of the sub-systems – produce changes in context for other context-dependent sub-systems. Changes in the context of a system may be incompatible with the maintenance of that system (its characteristic structures and processes, which give it identity).
17. Capitalists control capital which is the basis of their control over relations of production, employment opportunities, and frequently special political prerogatives. These derived control links are in part a function of the definition of property rights, but can also be the result, for instance, of ideological justification and social norms.
18. Incompatible processes may have the character of dominant and recessive tendencies which are simultaneously embodied in a particular social system or its different sub-systems. Dialectically transformative restructurings, somewhat like Hegelian syntheses, may then be thought of as relatively sudden switches in positions of dominance of such co-occurring tendencies or organizing principles.
19. The development of social systems (and their institutions) depends to a substantial degree on two basic dialectical relationships: the relationship between human societies and nature, or the physical or biological environments on which societies depend; and the dialectical relationships between actors in and between societies. Mankind's necessary contacts with his natural environment creates the conditions for its environment to shape him, through shaping, to some degree, his action and interaction possibilities and experience. But, in turn, human consciousness and activity shape the natural environment, often in unintended ways.
20. Reproducing an institution, even if it is limited to a particular sphere, depends on conditions and developments in other spheres and sub-systems.
21. Such power shifts may be initiated in a variety of ways. All have in common the failure of existing institutional arrangements and dominant groups to fully control innovations, resource distributions, and development of action capabilities which are incompatible with the existing social structure and systems of social action. These developments often occur as a result of events or changes external to the system but also emerge through the logic of internal system development, that is, where the 'seeds of destruction' are contained within the existing system, for instance in the case of system growth leading to resource exhaustion and shifts in control over remaining resources (Burns, 1976).
22. Ideologies and models of social action and interaction reflect and represent to a greater or lesser degree the environment on which humans act, e.g. the physical and social worlds. They also constitute means or sources of guidelines to act on them as well as to structure and transform them. In particular, they contribute to the structuring of systems of social action. But social action may, in turn, alter the physical and social environments leading to conditions and processes which contradict the model that gave rise to such action in the first place.

One of the characteristic features of praxis is that theory in action becomes a social and material force. In this sense. Durkheim's view of 'ideas as forces' is a valid one. Once they enter into human knowledge and 'consciousness', they affect beliefs, goals, and actions. In this way, they become 'real', that is *social facts*. Thus, once any 'adequate' representation of the world has been developed, it may dialectically abolish itself as a reflection of reality by transforming reality through action (Murphy, 1971).

Often ideology may be formulated and used by ruling groups and their spokesmen in such a way as to suggest 'unreal' states of the social system so as to provide disadvantaged groups with incorrect models of the system. This tends to weaken or confuse any restructuring attempts on their part, and reduces threats to system reproduction.

23. Much of contemporary social science methodology is predicated on the assumption of closed, morphostatic (structure maintaining) systems for which 'general principles', 'laws', and 'functional relationships' are invariant. That is, fixed (or 'stable') causal structures are assumed (Baumgartner et al., 1976a, 1977a). Social science data collection and analysis are often limited to a time span of observation chosen so that the morphogenic potentialities and developments of social systems are not detectable (that is, relationships between and among variables appear stable). Or, if the time span allows such detection, the models in which data are used tend to ignore instability. In many instances, the very choice of time frame and research setting will determine whether or not, and to what degree, there is apparent system closure and structural stability.

References

Alker, H., Jr., T. Baumgartner and T. R. Burns, 'Center/Periphery Relationships in the World System.' *Alternatives: A Journal of World Policy*, 1978.

Alker, H., Jr., W. Buckley and T. R. Burns, 'Introduction and Overview.' In: T. R. Burns and W. Buckley (eds.), *Power and Control: Social Structures and Their Transformation*. London and Beverly Hills: Sage, 1976.

Ashby, W. R., *An Introduction to Cybernetics*. New York: Wiley, 1957.

Baumgartner, T., *The Political Economy of International Economic Exchange and Development: A Systems Approach to the Structuring of the International Economic System*. Ph.D. Dissertation. University of New Hampshire: Durham, New Hampshire, 1976.

Baumgartner, T., and T. R. Burns, *Wildcat Strikes: The Cases of Sweden and Switzerland*. Scandinavian Institutes of Administrative Research. Research Report. Lund, Sweden, 1977.

Baumgartner, T and T. R. Burns, 'The Structuring of International Economic Relations.' *International Studies Quarterly*, 19:126-159, 1975.

Baumgartner, T., T. R. Burns and P. DeVillé, 'Work, Politics and Structuring under Capitalism.' In T. R. Burns, L. E. Karlsson and V. Rus (eds.), *The Liberation of Work and Political Power*. London: Sage, 1978a.

Baumgartner, T., T. R. Burns and D. Sekulic, 'Self-Management, Markets and Political Institutions in Conflict.' In T. R. Burns, L. E. Karlsson and V. Rus (eds.), *op cit*., 1978b.

Baumgartner, T., T. R. Burns and P. DeVillé, 'Conflict Resolution and Conflict Development: A Theory of Game Restructuring with an Application to the LIP Conflict.' In L. Kriesberg (ed.), *Research in Social Movements, Conflict and Change*. Greenwich: JAI, 1978c.

Baumgartner, T., T. R. Burns and D. Meeker, 'The Description and Analysis of System Stability and Transformation: Multi-Level Concepts and Methodology.' *Quality and Quantity*, 1977a.

Baumgartner, T., T. R. Burns and P. DeVillé, 'The Oil Crisis and the Emerging World Order: The Structuring of Institutions and Rule-Making in the International System.' *Alternatives: A Journal of World Policy*, 3:75-108, 1977b.

Baumgartner T., T. R. Burns and P. DeVillé, 'Autogestion and Planning: Dilemmas and Possibilities.' Paper presented at the Second International Conference on Participation, Worker's Control and Self-Management. Paris, 1977c.

Baumgartner, T., T. R. Burns and P. DeVillé, 'Divide et Impera.' Unpublished manuscript, 1977d.

Baumgartner, T., T. R. Burns, D. Meeker and B. Wild, 'Open Systems and Multi-Level Processes: Implications for Social Research.' *Int. J. of General Systems*, 3:25-42, 1976a.

Baumgartner, T., W. Buckley, T. R. Burns and P. Schuster, 'Meta-power and the Structuring of Social Hierarchies.' In: T. R. Burns and W. Buckley (eds.) *Power and Control*. London and Beverly Hills: Sage, 1976b.

Baumgartner, T., W. Buckley and T. R. Burns, 'Unequal Exchange and Uneven Development.' *Studies in Comparative International Development*, 11:51-72, 1976c.

Baumgartner, T., T. R. Burns, P. DeVillé and D. Meeker, 'A Systems Model of Conflict and Change in Planning Systems.' *General Systems Yearbook*, 20:167-183, 1975a.

Baumgartner, T., T. R. Burns and P. DeVillé, 'Middle East Scenarios and International Restructuring: Conflict and Challenge.' *Bulletin of Peace Proposals*, 6:364-378, 1975b.

Baumgartner, T., W. Buckley and T. R. Burns, 'Relational Control: The Human Structuring of Cooperation and Conflict.' *Journal of Conflict Resolution*, 19:417-440, 1975c.

Baumgartner, T., W. Buckley and T. R. Burns, 'Meta-power and Relational Control in Social Life.' *Social Science Information*, 14:49-78, 1975d.

Buckley, W., *Sociology and Modern Systems Theory*. Englewood Cliffs: Prentice-Hall, 1967.

Buckley, W., (ed.), *Modern Systems Research for the Behavioral Scientist*. Chicago: Aldine, 1968.

Buckley, W., T. R. Burns and D. Meeker, 'Structural Resolutions of Collective Action Problems.' *Behavioral Science*, 19:277-297, 1974.

Burns, T. R., 'Unequal Exchange and Uneven Development in Social Life: Continuities in a Structural Theory of Social Exchange. *Acta Sociologica*, 20:217-245, 1977.

Burns, T. R., *Dialectics of Social Systems: Their Reproduction and Transformation*. Working Papers Nr. 50. Oslo: University of Oslo, Institute of Sociology, 1976.

Burns, T. R. and W. Buckley, 'The Prisoners' Dilemma Game as a System of Social Domination.' *J. of Peace Research*, 11:221-228, 1974.

Burns, T. R. and D. Meeker, 'Conflict and Structure in Multi-Level, Multiple Objective Decision-Making Systems.' In C. A. Hooker (ed.), *Foundations and Applications of Decision Theory*. Dordrecht, Holland: Reidel, 1977.

Caneiro, R. L., 'A Theory of the Origin of the State.' *Science*, 169:733-738, 1970.

Coleman, J. S., *Community Confict*. Glencoe, Ill.: Free Press, 1957.

Deutsch, K. W., *The Nerves of Government*, 1963.

Deutsch, M., *The Resolution of Conflict: Constructive and Destructive Processes*. New Haven and London: Yale University Press, 1973.

DeVillé, P. and T. R. Burns, 'Institutional Responses to Crisis in Capitalist Development: A Dialectical Systems Approach.' *Social Praxis*, 4:5-46, 1977.

Finer, S., 'State Building, State Boundaries, and Border Control.' *Social Science Inform.*, 13:79-126, 1975.

Geyer, R. F., 'Individual Alienation and Information Processing: A Systems Theoretical-Conceptualization.' In: R. F. Geyer and D. Schweitzer (eds.), *Theories of Alienation – Critical Perspectives in Philosophy and the Social Sciences*. The Hague: Martinus Nijhof, pp. 189-223, 1977.

Geyer, R. F., 'Alienation and General Systems Theory.' *Sociologia Neerlandica*, X:18-40, 1974.

Godelier, M., *Rationality and Irrationality in Economics*. New York: Monthly Review, 1973.

Hardin, H., 'Stability of Statist Regimes: Industrialization and Institutionalization.' In T. R. Burns and W. Buckley (eds.), *Power and Control*. London: Sage, pp. 147-168, 1976.

Herbst, P., *Behavioral Worlds*. London: Tavistock, 1971.

Hirschman, A. O., *Exit, Voice and Loyalty*. Cambridge: Harvard University Press, 1970.

Katz, D. and R. Kahn, *The Social Psychology of Organizations*. New York: Wiley, 1966.

Kriesberg, L., *Sociology of Social Conflicts*. Englewood Cliffs, N.J.: Prentice-Hall, 1973.

Luce, R. D. and H. Raiffa, *Games and Decisions*. New York: Wiley, 1957.

Murphy, R., *The Dialectics of Social Life*. New York: Basic Books, 1971.

Rapoport, A., *Fights, Games and Debates*. Ann Arbor: U. of Michigan Press, 1960.

Schuhmacher, E. F., *Small is Beautiful*. New York: Harper & Row, 1973.
Simmel, G., *The Sociology of Georg Simmel* (edited by K. H. Wolff). New York: Free Press, 1964.
Von Neumann, J. and O. Morgenstern, *Theory of Games and Economic Behavior*, 3rd. ed. Princeton, N.J.: Princeton University Press, 1953.
Zeitlin, I., *Rethinking Sociology: A Critique of Contemporaty Theory*. Englewood Cliffs, N. J.: Prentice-Hall, 1973.

An actor-oriented systems model for the analysis of industrial democracy measures

Tom Baumgartner

1. Introduction

The paper 'Actors,games and systems' by Baumgartner, Burns and De Villé in this volume outlines the theoretical perspective of an actor-oriented systems analysis. This paper here is an outgrowth of that general research effort to model and analyze the structuring and restructuring of social systems. The paper focuses in particular on the visual representation of key concepts of this actor-oriented systems analysis. This modelling exercise involves a simple model of a capitalist system designed to assess the restructuring potential of forms and reforms of work organisation commonly known as industrial democracy measures.[1]

Of course, both the theoretical base and practical conception of an actor-oriented systems approach as well as the specific characterization of the capitalist system used here are subject to debate. But the primary intent of this paper is to discuss the translation of systems concepts and verbal descriptions of a complex system into a visual model. This model has been designed foremost for expositional and illustrative purposes. It is certainly not, at least not at this stage, a prototype for or a precursor to a 'scientific', i.e. numerical, simulation model.

The plan of the paper is the following. Section 2 recalls the key concepts of the actor-oriented systems approach which, however, are more fully developed in the aforementioned paper included in this volume. Section 3 presents the visual conceptualization of an economic production and exchange process. Section 4 discusses the modelling of interlinkages between the economic, socio-cultural and political spheres of the capitalist system as sources of systems reproduction. Section 5 uses the model to discuss subsystem correspondence as a factor in the reproduction and transformation potential of a capitalist system in the face of industrial democracy reforms.

2. The conception of a social action system

The analysis of reproduction and transformation processes in complex social systems makes use of three basic concepts:[2]

- the multi-dimensionality of social processes and their outcomes;
- the spin-off and spill-over effects of social production and exchange;
- and the multi-level linkages between processes and spheres of social action.

As a consequence, spheres or subsystems of a social system are linked with each other through a complex set of interdependencies, flows and interrelationships. Actors belong at one and the same time to different spheres of social action and do so in different capacities and as members of various classes and groups. Actions and processes in one sphere generate multiple outputs and outcomes, including the spin-off and spill-over effects, which link different actions and processes among themselves within the sphere as well as with those in other spheres. Actions and processes are also utilizing inputs coming from within and without their sphere.

But above all, actions and processes take place in a context. Economic production and exchange is constrained by political and sociocultural factors, rules, norms, guiding concepts and assumptions. Similarly, political action is limited by economic potential and feasibility. The products of actions and processes in turn can modify the constraints operating on a given subsystem, system component, or element. Actions and processes are therefore linked to one another not only in the usual causal relationships and feedback loops, but also through structuring linkages and processes. These are operators on processes, functions, and relationships rather than on variables. They represent in this sense higher-order, that is, meta-forms of determination or causality.

Actors exercise property and, more generally, control rights over valuables and processes. They occupy differentiated positions in the structure of relationships and exercise different roles in the social division of action. They have therefore qualitatively and quantitatively different relationships to the products (including the spin-offs and spill-overs) of social action. It is this variation in control, hence of power and meta-power, which leads to uneven accumulation processes and the unequal development of actors' capabilities. Baumgartner, Burns and DeVillé suggest in their paper (in this volume) that the confluence of different interests and goals with differentiated power and meta-power positions of actors and classes of actors generates structuring and restructuring forces within the complexity of a social system which is only partially integrated.

Structuring and restructuring forces will in general transform the system in the absence, on the part of dominant actors and classes of actors, of conscious and successful structuring activity oriented toward the reproduction of essential system characteristics. Industrial democracy reforms are designed to resolve various dysfunctionalities of the capitalist organization of work and work relations.[3] Therefore the approach and model here presented lend themselves well to considering the reproductive or possibly transformative potential of such industrial democracy reforms.

3. Production and distribution processes

Production and exchange processes are central to the reproduction and transformation potential of social systems. The analysis starts therefore with the presentation of a basic production and exchange model for the economic sphere. The analysis will then be expanded to consider production and exchange in the context of the economic sphere. This type of analysis is also applied to production and distribution processes in the socio-cultural sphere.

3.1. The labor-wage exchange system

The economic production and exchange process represented in the model of Figure 1 incorporates three structural and institutional characteristics which are basic to capitalistically organized production and exchange activities:

- The complex relations of production whereby the actors or classes of actors in the system – the owners and managers [*A*] of capital and the workers [*B*] as sellers of labor power – are differentiated in their power and control possibilities at the same time that they are bound together in a structured system or totality.
- The differentiation in function between the owners and managers of capital and the sellers of labor power. The former use power based on control over, and technical knowledge about, the means of production in order to plan, structure, and manage the production process, the type of technology employed, the organization of work and work processes, etc. Workers and employees submit their labor power to be directed and

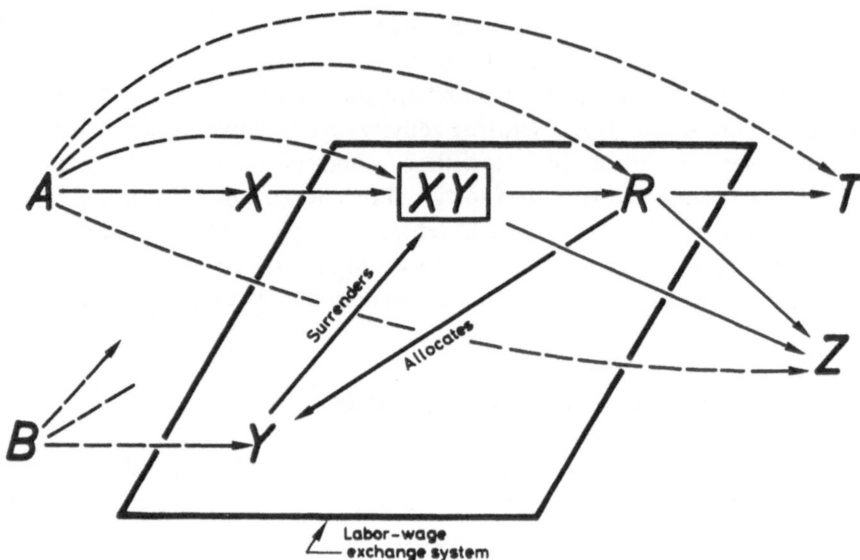

Figure 1. Structure of an economic production and exchange process

Key: Actors and valuables		*Signs*	
A	Capitalists and managers	*XY*→*R*	Flow of production
B	Worksers	*A*-→*X*	Exercise of dominant control
Y	Labor power		
X	Means of production	*B*-→*X*	Exercise of subordinate control
XY	Process of production		
R	Production output, revenue	*R*→*Y*	Exchange process
T	Transfers	☐	Process context
Z	Knowledge, skills, information		

managed as part of the total process of production.

- The differentiation in gains and losses among actors or classes of actors participating in the production and distribution system, e.g. leaving [*B*] with control over labor income while [*A*] controls profits as well as many other products and values generated in the course of production and interaction with the environment of the enterprise.

Figure 1 represents such an unevenly structured situation. Employers [*A*] control the means of production (*X*) as well as the process (*XY*) of combining them with the purchased labor power (*Y*). They also control the direct output from this process of production and the revenues (*R*) realized through selling it on the market.[4] Of course, part of (*R*) has to be allocated as labor income to the workers [*B*] for their reproduction of (*Y*). Part of (*R*) is leaving the production and exchange system as taxes and other transfer payments (*T*). (Of course, (*T*) comes ultimately back again in the form of governmental payments, subsidies, etc.) In addition; [*A*] exercises sole control over (*Z*) derived both from the production process itself, as well as from the generation of output, revenue and profits.[5] (*Z*) can be understood as managerial knowledge and capabilities, information about the larger economic as well as the other spheres of the social system, consumer and worker attitudes, etc. As we will see, these valuables are important inputs into political and social processes. And these in turn play a great role in the reproduction of the economic sphere itself.

Control is indicated in Figure 1 with broken arrows linking actors exercising control to entities controlled. This control can be over a given valuable, e.g. (*X*) or (*R*), or over a constraining context, symbolized here as a box enclosing a process, for example, the production process (*XY*). In this case, control implies the possession of meta-power by [*A*] (see Section 3.3 of the paper by Baumgartner, Burns and DeVillé). That is, [*A*] has the right and the capability to organize the production process according to his designs. This includes such things as controlling the workers' access to information, knowledge, and capability acquisition, the provision of safe and sound working environments, trade union and political activity within the enterprise, etc. It also implies the possibility to manipulate pay-off structures (in addition to wage payments) by organizing promotional opportunities or assigning pleasant and easy work tasks. And finally, [*A*] has the right to organize work positions in such a way that individual workers or groups of workers are kept isolated from each other, In short, [*A*] can divide [*B*] in order to better control them.[6]

Workers [*B*] are essentially restricted to controlling their labor power (*Y*), which they have however to surrender to [*A*] in exchange for a part of (*R*). This labor income (*r*) (see Figure 2) has to be used for the reproduction of laborpower through consumption, a process which too is largely under the control of [*B*] (but see Note 4). But consumption does not provide any long-term benefits, and, above all, does not provide any structuring power. Of course, [*B*] exercises under modern political and social conditions some control over various valuables and processes formerly totally controlled by [*A*]. But this control is never a dominant one, remains partial, intermittent, and has often to be exercised indirectly through managerially and technocratically oriented representatives. Workers in different countries have for example acquired some capital ownership through various funds. They have also fought for and gained the right to control and limit the exercise of absolute control by [*A*] over the organization of the work process (*XY*). This situation is indicated in Figure 1 by short control links going from [*B*] in the direction of (*X*) and (*XY*) without however linking up with them. That is, control is not even shared by [*B*] with [*A*], but clearly remains subordinate to the control of [*A*].

This analysis is of course structurally and temporarily oversimplified. It fails to take account of 'contradictory class locations' (Wright, 1976) as well as center-periphery differentiations. In considering these more elaborate social structures and the structural developments based on them, one makes use of the same theoretical perspective and arguments developed here and in Baumgartner, Burns and DeVillé in this volume.

For instance, technocrats are an emergent group of increasing importance. Their relationship to the means of production is typically not one of ownership. But they occupy by virtue of their knowledge, skills and education relatively high positions in authority hierarchies. They often exercise actual economic ownership over the means of production and the production process thanks to their strategic positions in the control structure over economic and technical processes. They belong therefore, or are closer to [*A*] (in Figures 1 or 2) than to [*B*]. Their control links to valuables and processes are substantially more important than those of [*B*]. At the present, technocrats operate *within* the institutional and ideological constraints of capitalism. However, their knowledge, skills, and their bargaining power based on their importance to the operation of the system puts them in a more favorable position than most non-[*A*] to get the system to serve their interests.[7]

The center-periphery analysis for example differentiates between two groups of [$A°$] and [*A*] which control different qualities of resources, including labor, which possess unequal action capabilities, and which enjoy typically different quantities and qualities of spin-offs and spill-overs ($R°$) and (*R*), ($T°$) and (*T*), etc. (see Figure 2). This analysis is more fully developed in Baumgartner et al. (1978a) for the case of the capitalist system, and is discussed with respect to the Yugoslav self-management system in Baumgartner et al. (1978b).

The social relationship between [*A*] and [*B*] represented in figure 1 is clearly marked by unequal access to and control over the means of production as well as the multiple social products of economic production and exchange.[8] These differences in resource control and action possibilities provide the basis for unequal exchange, and a process of uneven accumulation and capability development (see Section 2.2 of Baumgartner, Burns and DeVillé in this volume).

[*A*] allocates to [*B*] in exchange for his or her labor power a certain income or certain goods (*r*) derived from the operation of the means of production. [*B*] has the right to use, as he sees fit, his income and other goods which he or she receives from the employer. But, in general, the resources [*B*] obtains offer only short-term, individualistic and consumptive benefits. [*A*] on the other hand gains control over goods, resources, and conditions which enhance his long-term action capabilities and structural advantages to continue the process of accumulation and to maintain and to reproduce the unequal or dependent relationship between [*A*] and [*B*]. Thus, workers create or contribute to the creation of resources and valuables for which they do not receive a share or do not get 'paid'.[9]

By means of gaining control over the economic and non-economic social products, (*XY*), (*R*), (*T*) and (*Z*), [*A*] gains in power relative to [*B*] as well as relative to other, more static groups in society associated with less dynamic and developing productive activities. This accumulation and extension process provides the basis of power in new economic domains as well as in political, administrative and socio-cultural spheres. It is this extension of power which helps in the structuring of the context within which economic production and exchange take place.

3.2. The context of economic production and exchange

Economic production and exchange take place, as suggested, within a certain institutional and structural context. This context is a produced, that is, a human construct and not a natural order. It has therefore to be continually reproduced. This involves, in part, the reproduction of the means of production and of labor power. This is indicated in the model (see Figure 2) by a loop from production of output and revenues (*R*) via labor income (*r*) to labor power (*Y*). A similar loop, here suppressed, would go from (*R*) to the means of production (*X*).

But reproduction also entails the continual structuring of the conditions and of the context of economic production and exchange so as to make and keep the context mutually compatible with the essential structures and processes of economic activity. This involves not only the enforcement of the various and unequally distributed property and control rights, but also the reproduction of appropriate norms and values across generations which

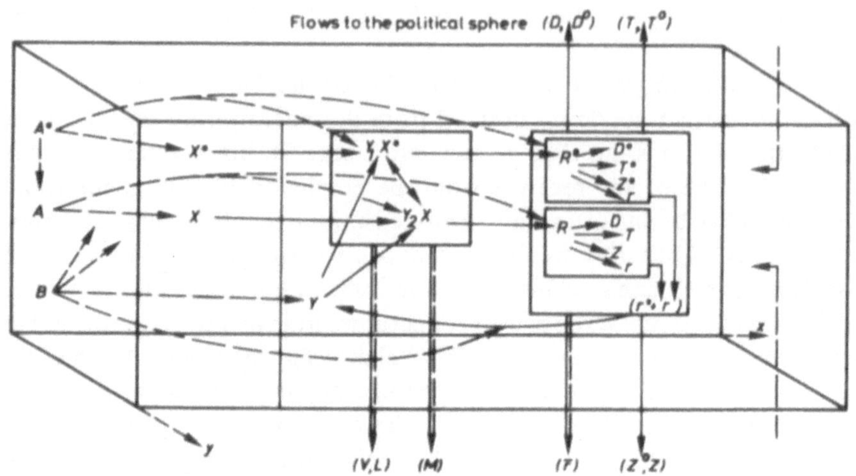

Figure 2. The context of economic production and distribution

Key:

$A°$	Capitalists/managers of center enterprises	r	Labor incomes (to center and periphery workers)
A	Capitalists/managers of periphery enterprises	$\bar{r}$	Relative labor incomes, income distribution
B	Workers (both in the center and periphery)	- - -→	Meta-level structuring processes
D, $D°$	Authority, expert status	⇒	Information and value flows between spheres
M	Management expertise		
V, L	Values, legitimation		

(For other symbols see Figure 1.)

are underpinning this structure of rights. It involves furthermore state activity to contain the uneven accumulation and development tendencies of a market system through a range of actions going from antitrust control activities to progressive taxation and welfare measures, or from the enforcement of health and safety norms to the subsidization of economic activity in peripheral regions and sectors (Baumgartner et al., 1978a). It implies the expenditure of much effort to solve the collective action problems so numerous in an individualistically oriented economic system.

All these various constraints and contextual conditions limiting the exercise of control by actors in the economic sphere over production and exchange processes are summarily and symbolically represented in the model by a box enveloping the production and exchange process and its various control relationships. This representation of context and its process in Figure 2 contains a more differentiated economic production and exchange process than modelled in Figure 1. As already mentioned, the model can differentiate between center and periphery enterprises [$A°$] and [A][10], and between material and financial outputs on one hand, and value and informational outputs on the other. In addition, Figure 2 includes flows from the economic production sphere to other spheres of social action as well as the structuring effects on the economic subsystem as a result of processes and outcomes in other spheres.

The planes of the contextual box stand for all the different contextual factors and elements defining the sphere: the constraints which shape relations of production and production processes.[11] Such contextual variables are for example property rights, laws, moral and ethical codes, social norms, etc. This context is defined by meta-level structuring processes and conditions. These are indicated in Figure 2 by the thick, broken lines contacting the right-hand (y, z)-plane of the box, and originating in other spheres of the system (see Figure 4).[12]

The left-hand (y, z)-plane contains the different classes and groups of actors. These too make up the context of the system. Their definitions and divisions are often the result of structuring processes, for example divide-and-rule strategies emanating from other spheres. It is clear that individuals can and do belong simultaneously to different groups and classes in a given sphere as well as in the other spheres. The previously evoked identity of [B] and consumers is one instance. But [B] is also a sum of political actors, if only in certain circumstances as an amorphous group of infrequent voters. These multiple identities reflect the multi-dimensional nature of social life. The linkages between the different categories and groups of actors, reflecting their different functions and interests in the economic, social and political spheres, are at the present left out of the analysis. But the particular structure, mapping actors and sets of actors in one sphere on to actors and sets of actors in other spheres is ultimately of great importance.

Not only would particular mapping structures indicate the non-economic goals, interests, values and considerations a given economic actor might take into account in his economic decision-making – because in taking decisions as economic actor, he would also be aware of his other capacities in the non-economic spheres.[13] But the mapping structure could also indicate the cohesiveness of a given class or group of actors in fighting for particular interests, e.g. through using their meta-power for structuring and restructuring activities. The political weakness of consumers, for example, is due to their diffused definition in the political sphere. Employers, on the other hand, have relatively uniform interests, at least at a higher level. These are often pushed through in the political sphere because of their cohesive organization, and of course, because of their control over important economic products, as indicated in Figure 1, which allows for particularly effective political action.

The upper and lower (x, y)-planes of the contextual box represent the process-level interfaces between the different spheres. They are a proper part of the context although they indicate the transit of process-level flows from one sphere to another. But the nature and extent of these flows are structured. These planes stand therefore for part of the sub-system integration and interdependency, or said differently, they represent degrees of subsystem autonomy and, hence, system robustness. That is, low levels of integration may make characteristic processes and structures of the different spheres less vulnerable to changes intervening in any one of the spheres (DeVillé and Burns, 1977).

The process-level interfaces are transited by material and immaterial flows: commodity, financial, as well as informational and value outputs of economic production and exchange processes are important inputs into political and socio-cultural processes. Of course, process-level outputs from the non-economic spheres transit similarly through the (x, y)-levels of the economic sphere (see Figure 4). That is, the (x, y)-levels express the multi-dimensionality of many economic processes and of their inputs and outputs.

It is also conceivable that control links exist between actors in one sphere and valuables and processes in other spheres. These are probably best conceived as process-level phenomena as long as they do not really affect the constraints on all classes or sub-classes of processes in a sphere.[14] The existence of such direct and pin-pointed control links is probably less common in a capitalist than in some other systems. But one example would be the governmental representative on the administrative board of nationalized or semi-public, but largely autonomous enterprises which are in general managed on the basis of traditional capitalist criteria. In contrast, such control links seem to be common in Yugoslavia under the social ownership concept reenforced with the 1972 constitution. There, self-managed enterprises determine through self-management agreements with communes, socio-political organizations and various user groups enterprise strategy and obligations (Baumgartner et al., 1978b).

The modelling of the other spheres of a social system is based on the same principles as the modelling of the economic sphere described here in some detail. Actors have differential control over processes and their various inputs and outputs. These processes take also place in a certain context which itself is the product of structuring forces and processes. The different spheres of a social system are therefore mutually linked both at the process and the structuring level.

Figure 3 represents a simple model of an educational process within the socio-cultural sphere. Such processes are very often also economic processes. What is here emphasized, however, is the socio-cultural nature of this processing of children and adults. Expository necessity forces one to disaggregate and separate economic and cultural spheres. But it should not be forgotten that what one tries to model here is the inherent multi-dimensionality of much of social activity.[15]

The socio-cultural aspect of an educational process is conceived here as involving an array of different actors, including an elite [*EL*] controlling the material inputs (*X*) as well as the school process as such.

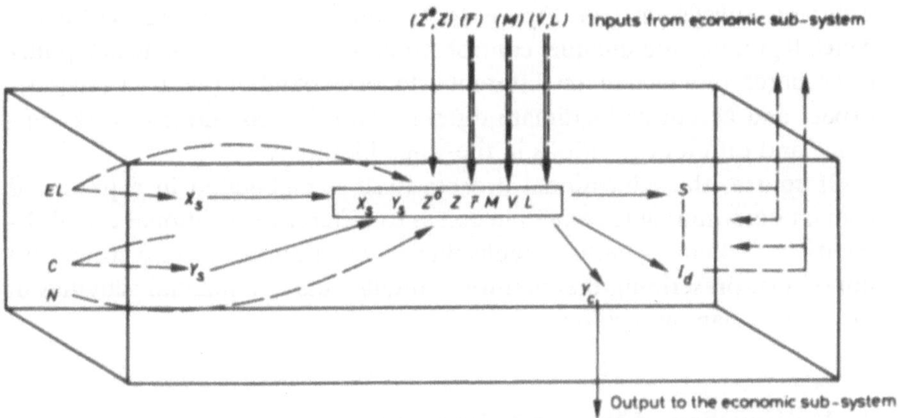

Figure 3. Structure and context of a socio-cultural production and distribution process

Key:

EL	Socio-cultural elite	*S*	Status distinctions
C	Consumers (students and parents)	I_d	Ideological values, norms
N	Outsiders	Y_c	Knowledge, skills, aptitudes, behavioral traits

(For other symbols, see Figures 1 and 2)

But in this case they have to share control over the school process with a group of outsiders [*N*] – outsiders in the sense that they are not members of the school establishment, nor parents or students. The consumers [C] of educational services, here to be conceived as both students and their parents, control of course their own labor as an important input into the process. They may also exercise some, but probably only partial and subsidiary control over the school process as such. Important inputs into this process are various process-level valuables originating in the economic sphere, e.g. the social identification of students according to their parents' position in the labor and income hierarchy (r), managerial expertise (M) acquired by elites in the economic production process and here applied to education and learning, as well as diverse values and legitimating factors (V, L) which originate in the business world and are to be absorbed by the students.

The outputs of this process are not only various categories of educated and trained labor (Y_c), i.e. categories of human capital, but also status distinctions and credentials (S) and shared values, ideological beliefs and social norms (I_d). (Y_c) can be envisaged as a process-level input into the economic subsystem (see Figure 4). (S) and (I_d) are structuring factors which legitimize the unequal control structures in the economic and political spheres, or which make different categories of labor (i.e. [$B°$] and [B]) expect and accept as legitimate different working conditions, work contents, and different positions in the wage hierarchy.

Of course, the educational process itself is embedded in a produced context determining for example access to different educational establishments and schooling paths, establishing control rights of certain groups but not others, prescribing the mixture of intellectual and manual activities in the school plan, and so on.

4. Reproduction of the capitalist system

The maintenance and reproduction of capitalist relations of production and processes depend on their socio-cultural and political contexts, just as the capitalist economy contributes to shaping processes and structures in the political and socio-cultural spheres. The discussion in the preceding section has indicated the complex forms such inter-sphere linkages may take. Of particular importance, of course, are the links between the political and economic spheres, and within this, the role of the state in regulating and controlling instability, uneven developments and conflicts.

Figure 4 provides a summary representation of the basic, but very selective, interrelationships, both at the process and the structure-level, between the economic, political and socio-cultural spheres. Consider the revenue (R) accruing to enterprises through their activities of producing and selling. Revenue is a complex factor. Its distribution links it as an input with various other spheres, including, of course, the economic sphere itself.[16] For example, the distribution of labor income ($\bar{r}$) shapes the life chances and consumption patterns of different occupational groups. Part of (R), the transfers (T), enter into the transactions between the economic and political spheres. The specific forms of (T) are many: tax and social security payments, bribes, contributions to election campaigns of politicians, in some systems the financing of interest groups charged with political lobbying on behalf of economic interests.[17] (T) is an input into the production process of political decisions insofar as the process itself consumes and requires resources (salaries, buildings, information systems, etc.). It is also an important input in the sense that many political decisions would remain empty if not backed by the allocation of the financial means for their realization, either for the purchase of human and material resources required in administrative activities, or for payment to other actors in the system.

Transfers (T) – and the production of them – provide a substantial legitimational aspect. The ability to produce increasing revenues and real resources for state activity, both for political production in the form of laws, decisions and financial allocations, and for the self-reproduction of the state administrative apparatus, offers one justification for the capitalist mode of production. This aspect of (T) – or maybe it is more meaningful to speak of this aspect of the economic sphere itself – contributes to structuring in a fundamental way the relationships between the economic and the other spheres of social action. Hence, the strong theoretical and practical arguments in favor of seeing the economic sphere as the dominant one.[18]

Revenue (R) assures the reproduction of labor and capital through the allocation of wages (r) to workers and depreciation to enterprises. But (r) are also incomes and they, and especially the relative incomes ($\bar{r}$), are inputs into social processes generating different action opportunities, life chances and status differentiation. That is, the distribution of income and wealth through capitalist relations of production contributes to the structuring of social differences in society (indicated, for example in Figure 4 with a structuring link from the economic to the socio-cultural sphere). At the same time, status differentiation (S) is an output of the socio-cultural subsystem and as such represents, as argued, a structuring factor of the

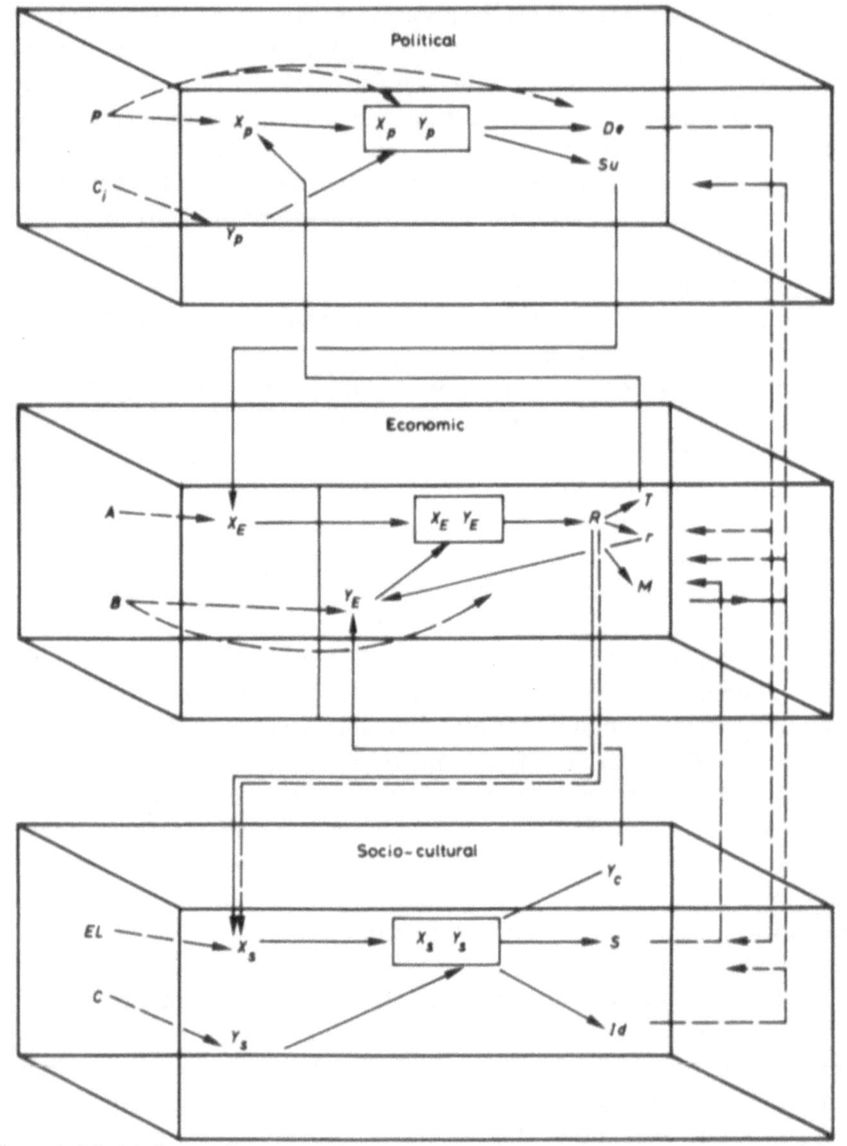

Figure 4. Model of a social system under capitalism with economic, socio-cultural and political spheres

Key:

P	Politicians	*De*	Decisions, laws
C_i	Citizens	*Su*	Financial allocations

(For other symbols, see Figures 1, 2, 3.)

economic sphere in terms of certain values, legitimation principles and social distinctions (I_d). These define appropriate standards of living and, hence, levels of income appropriate for different actor categories. They make certain structures of function and of wages appear as 'fair' or socially acceptable as in the allocation of (*R*) between managers and capitalists [*A*], and workers [*B*], or among workers according to occupation, sex, religion, ethnicity and race.[19]

The control of the economic system of production and distribution by [*A*] implies that this actor is able to intervene and to influence events and developments in other spheres. This is accomplished not only through the use of real resources (*T*) and of the authority (*D*) derived from expertise and from successful economic activity, but also through controlling evaluation criteria, legitimating results, and related developments associated with production processes. For instance, managers structure the division of labor, that is, the way in which jobs and functions are allocated, above all between physical, and between managerial and mental work. This is not only an organization of production for economic and technical purposes.[20] It produces and reproduces the unequal distribution of technical and managerial knowledge and skills (*M*) which are particularly important bases for social hierarchy formation in modern societies and provide the justification for unequal control and participation in political processes.

The structuring of the production process limits the possibilities of the workers [*B*] for the development and acquisition of (*M*). The underdevelopment of labor in this and related aspects assures not only continued subordination to a technocratic elite in the work place – i.e. a structuring link from and to the economic sphere itself – but also its subordination in political and socio-cultural spheres – a structuring link from the economic to the other spheres. In this way, the structuring of the production process contributes to the reproduction of work relations in other spheres. Moreover, the underdevelopment of labor makes for relatively weaker language and cognitive training and is reproduced in working-class children both through pre-school family socialization and the school process itself. As suggested, this reproduces class relations intergenerationally and maintains the particular relations of production which are at their origin in the first place.

But other mutual reenforcement loops exist between conditions and developments in the economic and the socio-cultural spheres. For instance, the use of certain types of technology may enhance the emergence of a technocratic value system. The decision to produce certain types of goods and not others affects social tastes and preferences. The privatization of consumption inhibits the development of group consciousness and collective organization, for example, among workers outside the workplace. And this condition too contributes to the reproduction of the unequal control structures so typically for the capitalist system.

5. Reproduction or transformation?

5.1. Subsystem correspondence and reproduction

The economic sphere partially shapes through resource and value transactions the socio-cultural and political context in which capitalist enterprises operate. In this way, socio-cultural and political processes mediate the self-reproducing structuring processes generated by the economic sphere. The effectiveness of these mediating effects depends on the compatibility of social structure and processes in the economy with those in the other spheres. The question is whether or not parallel or similar hierarchical systems obtain. Resource, information, and value production in the economic sphere will play an effective role in reinforcing and reproducing capitalist production relations provided that structures and processes in the other spheres (i.e. its context) are concordant or compatible. Structural correspondence enhances the effectiveness of resource transfers and value and norm processes. This is the key factor in the reproduction of the system as a whole.

Inputs into political and socio-cultural production are not entirely controlled by capitalists and managers [*A*]. To the extent that workers [*B*] can and do produce their own political and socio-cultural organizations – because they have resources available for such purposes – one may observe the phenomenon of the displacement of conflict processes from one sphere of social action to others. The conflictual relationship between [*A*] and [*B*] is then reproduced in other spheres, although the formal actors involved might be defined differently in the various spheres. Whatever the degree of arbitrariness of labels like voters, citizens, and lobbies, or elites, consumers, the elderly, the young, and different ethnic groups, they indicate that social actors structure and identify themselves differently in relation to different spheres of social action. At the same time there may be considerable overlap in terms of the individuals and groups involved.

In sum, the dominance relationships, concepts and values associated with capitalist production may not be realized or find compatible parallels in the political and socio-cultural spheres. On the contrary, they may be contradicted, e.g. opposed by actors committed to articulating and realizing, through social, cultural and political struggles, democratic norms and the humanization of work. Such opposition may contribute through industrial democracy reforms to some restructuring of capitalist forms of organizing production. This is not to say that these reforms transform capitalist relations.

On what conditions or factors does structural concordance – or its absence – depend?

1. The greater the overlap of elites, the more likely structural concordance will obtain. At the present, the conflictive relationship between capitalists and workers is only weakly, if at all, reproduced in the socio-cultural sphere. Thus workers (as consumers and citizens) have few opportunities or even incentives to form sentiments of solidarity and to organize outside of the workplace. In particular, their impact on educational, research, and national and international communication and information systems is minimal, although activities and developments in these areas influence substantially societal development.
2. High consensus and overlap or network ties between elites in economic, socio-cultural and political spheres is conducive to reproduction. Significant differentiation and incongruence may threaten it. Such situations give rise to alternative or competing bases of elite legitimation, to polarization of elites, and to a reduction in their ability to cooperate in adapting or bringing about non-basic restructuring of the system in response to crises or external challenge. In a word, meta-power disequilibrium obtains.
3. Inputs into the socio-cultural production processes are not only the material resources, values and information from the economic sphere. Conflicting values, beliefs, legitimations, tastes and preferences are produced and structured through a number of other processes: through socialization, traditions, customs and conventions; through religious beliefs and practices; through the perceptions that actors have of their positions and changes in them within the social system; through conflict processes within the different spheres. These multiple and alternative inputs into the socio-cultural production process are thus not completely determined by the economic sphere. They may thus work in opposition to the conditions which provide for the reproduction of economic relations and processes. Moreover, the economic relations and processes

themselves may generate conditions which are in opposition to their reproduction and further development. The reproduction of capitalist relations is made difficult in the face of strong democratic and egalitarian norms and values. That is, there exists a certain incompatibility between the hierarchically ordered structures and processes in the economic sphere and the democratic pretensions with respect to structures and processes in the political sphere.

It can now be seen more clearly under what conditions structuring or meta-processes between spheres of social action might contribute to morphogenic and transformative tendencies on the one hand, and, on the other, to stability and reproduction of the system. To exemplify this, let us take the extremely simple case where structural concordance between conflictual relationships and processes in two spheres is substantial. For instance, elites [*EL*] in the socio-cultural sphere are high status, high income groups closely linked with managerial and capitalist elites [*A*]. Consumers [*C*] are closely related to dominated production groups and workers [*B*]. To the extent that [*A*] controls the resource transfers and the value flows – at the same time that [*EL*] controls the key conditions and inputs of the socio-cultural sphere relevant to the structuring of the economic system – to that extent the outputs, such as the technocratic values and status differentiations, of the socio-cultural system will tend to be compatible with the reproduction of both itself and the economic subsystem. This compatibility reflects the concordance of relationships and processes in the two spheres with respect to the unequal distribution of power between the elites and the workers/consumers, and between the outputs of the two production processes.

5.2. Industrial democracy reforms: system maintaining or system transforming strategies?

The question to be asked about industrial democracy reforms in the light of the above considerations is to what extent do they provide workers with structuring and restructuring capabilities. The model described here translates this into two more specific questions:

- To what extent does a reform restructure control relationships within the capitalist enterprise (see Figures 1 and 2)?
- And to what extent does increased control by workers over their labor and labor process allow them to extend their control and power to other spheres of social life (see Figure 4)?

The preceding discussion suggests the following answers:

1. Most industrial democracy reforms cannot be assessed favorably. Reforms such as *Mitbestimmung*, co-determination and the like represent only increased influence, not extensive control (either in the legal or the technical sense) over relations of production, production processes, and products. Even changes in power relationships around the production process, e.g. through workers' acquisition of participatory decision-making rights, typically leave meta-power distribution unchanged. That is, the power to structure power relationships between managers and workers in the enterprise, to restructure the production process, or the relationships to other actors and processes in the environment remain managerial prerogatives.

   Thus the analysis implies that it is essential to specify and assess the level (or levels) at which a reform may affect the social system. The reproductive potential of the system is unlikely to be weakened if power redistribution is limited to the process-level as opposed to redistribution of meta-power at the structural level.

2. There may be indirect changes in the distribution of power and control mediated through political and socio-cultural processes. Thus, reforms introduced in work organizations, although they have a minimal direct impact on the distribution of power and meta-power, can have structuring effects on such organizations through their influence on political and sociocultural productions. For instance, worker representation on the board of directors of enterprises has had a minimal impact on enterprise management and control. Nevertheless, important socio-cultural and political implications can develop over the long run through changes in the public image of workers and labor union leaders, of their role in industrial life and, hence, their future roles in the wider system. Workers themselves and the public will develop new conceptions about the feasibility and appropriateness of worker participation in all kinds of decision-making processes as they discover and develop their capacity to make decisions. The acquisition of new skills, knowledge and attitudes will enhance political participation and this will most likely lead to new goals and demands, the perception of new action possibilities and potentialities for change.

   But these ramifications and developments are unlikely to be forthcoming in contexts where access to and influence over educational and informational facilities and processes by workers and their representatives remain restricted. In general, one would expect that the same measure leads to different outcomes in different political and socio-cultural contexts. For this reason, the argument for indirect and derived change effects of a given reform must be traced and analyzed in the different spheres of social life and at the different levels. Only in this way can one judge the ultimate potential of a reform measure.

3. The creation of participatory structures and processes at various levels does provide new platforms for individual and collective expressions by workers. However, past experience in industrialized capitalist countries seems to indicate that participation is accompanied by integration and not emancipation of workers.[21] This may be less a function of the participatory arrangement as such, but it may result from the use of the same action criteria and constraints dominating a managerially controlled economy. Thus, one should be led to explore the possibility of changing the dominant ideology and logic of evaluation, decision-making and social action in production processes together with changing the power relations as such. This suggests the importance of struggle and innovation in the socio-cultural sphere itself. Of specific concern here should be the development of alternative concepts, information and accounting systems, technology, forms and processes of work, all able to contribute to emancipatory processes in general.
4. Many industrial democracy reforms are major achievements for workers in that they contribute to maintain the physical and mental health and the security of workers. Moreover, such changes, which are valuable *per se*, can also contribute to change concepts and norms regarding the nature of work, work processes and work environments. Such socio-cultural changes have a structural impact over the long run.

6. Conclusion

The analysis and model proposed here has been limited to the consideration of a few key resource, value and knowledge flows, and the strategic structuring and contextual interlinkages between the economic, socio-cultural and political subsystems of a capitalist system. The application of this perspective to an evaluation of industrial democracy measures suggests that they do not provide workers with an extensive set of powers and meta-powers. In this sense, these reforms can be judged as structure maintaining changes.

To go beyond system maintaining and reproducing functions, reforms would have to involve changes in multiple spheres. The liberation of work requires activity not only in the economic but also in the political and socio-cultural spheres. Only in this way will be produced institutional conditions and rules as well as concepts, norms and values which facilitate the establishment of democratic control over work. Moreover, this would contribute to the development of democratic concepts and practices in all the other spheres of social action.

In addition, the desired fundamental change in the natureof work entails complementary action at multiple levels.[22] This would involve, for one, the extension of workers' control at the enterprise over the process of production and its multiple products and outcomes. But it also would have to include extension of control and influence over the structuring activities determining the political, legal and socio-cultural context within which enterprises and work organizations operate.

Notes

1. The results reported here are based on joint work with Tom R. Burns and Philippe DeVillé. Important features of the model have greatly benefited from the design capabilities of P. DeVillé. However, I alone remain responsible for the uses made here of the materials from our joint research.
2. Readers should consult the paper by Baumgartner, Burns and DeVillé in this volume for a more complete presentation of the theoretical perspective underlying these concepts.
3. See for example the analysis of monetary and financial systems restructuring in DeVillé and Burns (1977) or of the conflictive management-labor relationship in Baumgartner et al. (1978c, 1975). Directly relevant to the present discussion are the detailed analysis of the restructuring potential of industrial democracy measures in Baumgartner et al. (1978a) and of the reproductive and transformative tendencies in the Yugoslav self-management system in Baumgartner et al. (1978b).
4. The model is simplistic insofar as it abstracts from consumers. But consumers are almost completely identical with [*B*], at least at this level of analysis. In addition, both consumers and workers do not have the option to exit from the system as such, but only to exercise voice (to use the metaphors of Hirschman (1970)). And finally, consumers are even less organized than workers and exert certainly almost minimal control and power over economic production and distribution processes. The non-inclusion of consumers should not hurt the analysis and the Galbraithian assumption of dominant control by [A] over (R) seems justified.
5. The representation of a sequential transformation of (*R*) into (*T*) and (*Z*) should not divert from the fact that some (*Z*) can represent other dimensions of (*R*).
6. Manipulation of action possibilities, pay-off structures, and social orientations are the three dimensions which structure a game situation (Burns and Buckley, 1974).
7. Okishio (1977) for example sees in this reallocation of control over information gathering, manipulation and use a fundamental threat to the present class organization of capitalist society.
8. The argument here refers ostensibly to contemporaty capitalist society. However, it can be extended with suitable modifications to industrial societies without significant private

ownership of the means of production. The argument applies wherever there is substantial differential control with a few actors making most of the key decisions and the remainder being subject to 'dependent participation'.

9. The products related to knowledge accumulation or skill development are not so much a matter of non-payment as a case of non-opportunity to gain them in production settings.
10. The micro-contexts, within which $[A^\circ]$ and $[A]$ operate, and which are indicated by the rectangles around (XY), are different for the two classes. For example, many laws regulating work processes, health and safety conditions, workers' participation, etc., do not apply to small enterprises and workshops. In some countries, Italy among others, these enterprises constitute a veritable 'black', i.e. illegal, sector.
11. A sphere consists of a hierarchy of contexts with distinct structuring and restructuring processes. The model makes abstraction from this subsuming all structuring influences in one, indistinct level.
12. It is also possible that a structuring process originates in the sphere whose context it affects. The political subsystem produces laws which regulate its own behavior.
13. Baumgartner, Burns and DeVillé in this volume argue that the actor-oriented systems approach does not assume 'rational' actors so dominant in economic theory. Rather conflicting interests, divided loyalties, non-pecuniary orientations in a world based on monetary calculations, non-comparabilities, etc., all contribute to undecideability, conflict, and decisions which look 'irrational' if looked at from the value-perspective of only one sphere.
14. Nor is it appropriate to consider the governmental representative on the board of directors of an autonomous nationalized enterprise (see text) as an economic actor to the extent that he makes felt purely political factors in enterprise decision-making.
15. It depends on the specific modelling purpose if a process acquiring knowledge is symbolized as one of the multiple outputs of the economic process, as is done in Figures 1 and 2, or if one models it as a separate, socio-cultural process being linked with the economic process because of the latter's multi-dimensionality.
16. These different aspects can indicate different level effects.
17. Some (T) are partly controlled through actors and outcomes of the political system. Taxes are a legal obligation (apart from the possibility of accounting manipulations).
18. This is difficult to depict graphically. It woud entail a flow linkage from (T) to the contour of the box containing all the spheres of the social system.
19. Managers staff positions, and allocate prerogatives and benefits based on general legitimacy principles and norms relating to status distinctions. Hyman and Brough (1975) argue that norms of fairness are social values which legitimize existing inequalities, disguise conflicts of interest, and buttress the position of those with power in society.
20. Social distinctions in the work place may not serve any technical need. Rather ideological and control functions may be at their basis.
21. This is certainly the case with autonomous work group reforms. Rasmus (1974) argues that job enrichment, autonomous work groups, and participation programs are generally designed to give workers greater responsibility for production without giving them independent control over the decisions that determine the context of production.
22. Of course, the history of the labor movement indicates just such multi-level and complementary activities to structure and regulate the conditions of work.

References

Baumgartner, T., T. R. Burns and P. DeVillé, 'Work, Politics and Social Structuring under Capitalism' in T. R. Burns, L. E. Karlsson and V. Rus (eds.), *The Liberation of Work and Political Power*, London: Sage, 1978a.

Baumgartner, T., T. R. Burns and D. Sekulic, 'Self-management, Markets and Political Institutions in Conflict' in T. R. Burns, L. E. Karlsson and V. Rus (eds.), *The Liberation of Work and Political Power*, London: Sage, 1978b.

Baumgartner, T., T. R. Burns and P. DeVillé, 'Conflict Resolution and Conflict Development'. In L. Kriesberg (ed.). *Research in Social Movements, Conflict and Change,* Greenwich, Conn., JAI Press, 1978c.

Baumgartner, T., T. R. Burns and W. Buckley, 'Relational Control: The Human Structuring of Cooperation and Conflict.' *Journal of Conflict Resolution* 19, 417-440, 1975.

Burns, T. R. and W. Buckley, 'The Prisoners' Dilemma Game as a System of Social Domination.' *Journal of Peace Research* 11, 221-228, 1974.

DeVillé, P. and T. R. Burns, 'Institutional Responses to Crisis in Capitalist Development.' *Social Praxis* 5, 1977.

Hirschman, A. O., *Exit, Voice and Loyalty*, Cambridge: Harvard University Press, 1970.

Hyman, R. and J. Brough, *Social Values and Industrial Relations*, Oxford: Blackwell, 1975.

Okishio, N., 'Notes on Technical progress and Capitalist Society.' *Cambridge Journal of Economics* 1, 93-100, 1977.

Rasmus, J., 'Why Management is Pushing "Job Enrichment".' *International Socialist Review*, December, 1974.

Wright, E. O., 'Class Boundaries in Advanced Capitalist Societies,'*New Left Review'*, No. 98, 3-41, 1976.

A theory of social change

Maria Nowakowska

1. Introduction

The aim of this paper is to suggest certain models which could be of some use in studying several important aspects of social change.

In the first sections, the considerations will concern the general problems of social dynamics which induce or oppose the change. Next, some psychological aspects will be treated, namely those of the choice of pro- or anti-social behaviour in a given situation, and with respect to a given social group.

Finally, a mathematical model will be presented, aimed at studying the problems of the dissemination of changes across the society.

2. Structure of the society

In order to be able to speak of social change, it is necessary to develop some means of describing the *state* of the society, that is, the object of the change.

A complete description of the state of the society would, naturally, involve an unmanageably large number of variables. Thus, it appears preferable to use an approach of 'stepwise' description: this consists of using those aspects which are relevant for the particular problems of analysis, neglecting all other aspects, at least initially, and enriching the description only at some later stages, as the need arises.

As already mentioned, the analysis in this paper will be concentrated mostly on two aspects: psychological ones, concerning the adoption or non-adoption of the rules of the group by an individual, and consequently, a choice of pro- or antisocial behaviour; and sociological ones, concerning the dissemination of some ideas across the society.

Formally, a description of the state of a society involves specification of at least the following seven objects:

$$\langle S, \mathscr{G}, C, f, \Pi, R, \sigma \rangle \tag{1}$$

Here S is simply a set of individuals under consideration, referred to as 'society'. Next, $\mathscr{G}$ is a class of nonempty subsets of S, its elements $G_1, G_2, \dots$ referred to as *social groups*. These groups need not be disjoint; particular examples, starting from the simplest groap, may be: the family of Mr. Smith; employees of a certain institution; a professional group, e.g. lawyers; members of a given political party, etc. The important point is that the groups in $\mathscr{G}$ form a number of hierarchical structures, ordered by the relation of inclusion.

The groups in $\mathscr{G}$ may in fact be fuzzy subsets of S (see Zadeh 1965), that is, for any given $G \in \mathscr{G}$ and $s \in S$, there may be given a degree of membership of s in G, ranging from 0 (non-membership) to 1 (complete membership), with intermediate values representing partial membership.

Next, C represents a set of certain goods, and $f: S \times C \rightarrow [0, \infty]$ is a function which to each $s \in S$ and $c \in C$ assigns a number $f(s, c)$ representing the share of person s in goods c.

The goods in C may be of various types. Thus, some goods are 'infinitely divisible', in the sense that they are not quantifiable, and that it is possible (at least in theory) to give them to all members of S. Typical examples here may be voting rights, constitutional rights, etc. The second category of goods are those which come in limited quantities; hence, giving them to some members of S restricts the possibility of giving them to other members of S. Examples here may be goods such as salaries, administrative positions, etc.

By concentrating the attention on goods of the first type only, it was possible to build (see Nowakowska, 1978) a formal theory of freedom; consideration of goods of both types, and of the forces behind the choice of a particular distribution f of goods, led to a formal theory of alienation (see Nowakowska, 1977, n.d.).

Before presenting the main ideas and results of these theories, let us introduce briefly the remaining concepts of the system (1). Thus, Π is a system of preference relations, one for each $s \in S$, over the class of all functions f, i.e. preferences over the ways the goods are distributed in the society. Thus, if f_1 and f_2 are two distributions of goods, then $f_1 \pi_s f_2$ means that s prefers distribution f_1 to distribution f_2. These preferences are assumed to be transitive and connected. For all f_1, f_2, f_3 and s:

$$\text{if } f_1 \pi_s f_1 \text{ and } f_2 \pi_s f_3, \text{ then } f_1 \pi_s f_3; \tag{2}$$

$$\text{either } f_1 \pi_s f_2 \text{ or } f_2 \pi_s f_1 \text{ (or both).} \tag{3}$$

In the usual manner, one may define the relations of indifference and strict preference of person s.

The preference system of person s is induced by his *valuations* of various goods; these valuations can be introduced explicitly in the system if there should be a direct need for doing so. For the purpose of the present study, however, it will be sufficient to operate with the concept of preference only.

The notion of preference allows us to introduce the concept of a *goal*, as a concept derived from π_s. This is quite straightforward if one restricts the considerations to one person and his goals. Then, a *possible goal* is any distribution f which is preferred by s to the actual distribution, say f_0, or – more generally – a class of such distributions. The goal may also be sometimes specified in terms of a class of distributions of goods which are less preferred to f_0, and in this case it will mean that the goal is to prevent a change from f_0 to some less desirable distribution of goods.

Naturally, in practice the goals are usually formulated verbally, without mentioning preferences explitly. The point is, however, that such goals can always be reduced to goals formulated in an equivalent way as a suitable set of distribution of goods, with an indication whether these distributions are to be achieved or avoided.

For instance, if one wants to have a larger share of some specific goods c_0, while preserving the shares of the remaining goods on at least the present level, then the goal will be described as the class of all distributions f such that:

$$f(s, c_0) > f_0(s, c_0)$$

and

$$f(s, c) \geq f_0(s, c) \text{ for all } c \neq c_0.$$

Of course, out of many goals which are possible, only some are actually pursued, i.e. the person s performs some actions to bring about these goals.

The situation becomes more complicated if one tries to define formally a goal of a group G, since the problem then arises of aggregating the system of preferences $\{\pi_s, s \in G\}$ into one preference, say π_G. As is well known (see Arrow, 1963), such an aggregation of preferences is possible only at the cost of resigning from some of the postulates of 'democracy' specified by Arrow.

As a way out of these complications a goal of the group G will therefore be defined (more realistically than by demanding once common preference system) as a set F_G of distributions of goods f. Roughly, the elements of F_G will be those f which comprise the relevant common features of preferences of members of G. To use an example, imagine that the goods in question are various positions in the government administration. Suppose that a group of persons G supports a presidential candidate A. Their individual preferences as regards distributions of persons among administrative positions differ, sometimes radically (e.g. if two persons in G compete for the same position). But the common feature of all preferences in π_G is that they put higher any distribution in which A is the president to distributions in which A is not the president.

Thus, each group G is characterized by one or more goals, π_G, π_G', π_G'', ... Naturally, the strength of a social group depends – in addition to a number of other factors – on the degree to which the individual preferences π_s of members of G agree with the goals π_G, π_G',..., and also agree among themselves.

The high degree of agreement of the first type corresponds to persons who are motivated to actively support the group, because their individual interests are identical, or nearly identical, with those of the group. The second type of agreement is necessary to minimize the internal rivalry and fights, which would weaken the group as a whole.

The next concept, R, is the set of *rules*, which operate within particular groups, restricting the behaviour of members of these groups. More precisely, these rules determine which behaviour is 'prosocial', or 'antisocial' with respect to the given group G.

In this context, 'prosociality' means intuitively undertaking such actions which increase the likelihood of occurrence of some functions f which belong to the goal π_G of the group; for antisociality the situation is just the opposite. It is worth remarking that the concepts of pro- and antisociality are relative to a given group G. Naturally, an important special case is that of prosociality (or antisociality) with respect to the whole society S.

Finally, σ is a binary relation in S, establishing the communication links between members of S. The assumptions about σ will be given in the following sections, which present a model of the dissemination of ideas in a society.

3. Social change

Given the description of the state of the society in the form of the system (1), i.e. specified by the set of persons S, group structure $\mathscr{G}$, goods C, distribution of goods f, preferences Π, rules R and communication network σ, one can consider social change, i.e. transitions to states in which at least one of the variables undergoes a change.

It is necessary to remark that the concept of social change is a fuzzy concept; indeed, it is not enough that *some* change occurs in system (1) to justify classifying it as a *social* change. For the latter, it is necessary that a change in one or more of the variables in (1) be *substantial*. The adjective 'substantial', naturally, reflects some inherent fuzziness as to the degree of change, above which one could justifiably classify it as a social change.

Now, the changes may be categorized depending on which of the seven variables is being transformed, and to what degree. The latter, i.e. the degree of the change, has to be specified in each instance by construction of an appropriate index, and the total change is measured by a suitable aggregation of these indices.

The most trivial change is that in the set S, and indeed, all other variables remaining invariant, it is doubtful whether any change in S alone would justify calling the change *social*.

Next, consider changes in the group structure $\mathscr{G}$. Here there are two basic types of changes, namely changes of membership in various groups with the basic structure of $\mathscr{G}$ invariant and changes in $\mathscr{G}$ in the sense of appearance of some new social groups, or disappearance of some other social groups. The first type of social change is exemplified, for instance, by a substantial increase of membership in some political party. The second would occur, for instance, with the appearance of a new political party, or a new faction of an old one, etc.

Next, changes may occur in the set of goods C. As before, one can distinguish here two types of change: appearance of new goods or disappearance of old ones and/or change of the amount of some goods to be distributed. The first type is exemplified by establishing a new institution which creates a certain number of vacant posts to be filled, the posts playing the role of goods. The second type of change occurs, e.g. in case an additional sum of money is to be allocated among the employees, etc.

Next, a change may concern the function f, describing the allocation of goods among the members of S. Here the number of possibilities is larger. To proceed systematically: the change may concern goods of the first type (non-quantifiable and infinitely divisible). In such cases, the social change means simply the change in the set of persons who have access to the goods in question. Giving the voting right to women may serve as an example here.

Another type of change occurs for 'binary' goods, such as administrative positions, when, for instance, the ruling party loses the election. Then the social change means simply filling the positions with nominees from the winning party.

Finally, for quantifiable goods, such as finances, the change means simply a change in allocation of money, e.g. some raises or cuts in salaries, etc.

The changes in distribution of goods f are the most 'visible' ones. As opposed to that, the changes in the preference system Π concern rather the domain of consciousness.

The change of preferences – or, equivalently, the change of individual or group goals – results in turn either from the change of valuations or from the change in the rules for aggregating multidimensional valuations.

Similarly, the change of rules R which operate within a social group concern rather the domain of consciousness. Here the change may concern addition of new rules, disappearance of the old ones, or simply change in the order of importance of the rules without a change in the set of these rules.

Finally, changes in σ, the communication network, may result from factors ranging from changes of organizational schemes within some institutions to changes of some social customs, or life patterns, which influence, for instance, the frequency of human contacts.

As already mentioned, to measure the change one would have to construct measures of the change along each of the 'dimensions', as specified by the variables in system (1), and then choose a way of aggregating these indices into one index of social change. There are, of course, many ways of constructing such an index; but unfortunately all of them are somewhat 'ad hoc'. Thus, suppose that $d_1, \ldots, d_7$ are indices measuring the changes along particular dimensions. Then, one could define ISC (index of social change) as $(\Sigma d_i^2)^{1/2}$, or $\Sigma a_i d_i$ for some $a_i > 0$, etc. or generally, ISC $= \Psi(d_1, \ldots, d_7)$, where Ψ is some increasing function.

4. A theory of freedom

Consider now only the goods of the first of the described types, i.e. goods which are not quantifiable, and such that (at least potentially) they may be given to any member of S. Then it may be assumed that the values of the allocation function f are only 0 and 1, representing non-participation and participation in the given goods.

In such a case, instead of f one may equivalently consider the family of sets:

$$C_s = \{c \in C : f(s,c) = 1\}$$

of goods which are allocated to person s.

If one now takes, as the considered goods, those which are related to freedom (voting rights, civil liberties, aristocratic privileges, etc.), then the sets $C_{s1}, C_{s2}, \ldots$ will describe the distribution of freedom in the society.

One can now define various notions relevant for the theory of freedom. Thus, *equality* with respect to a set $C' \subset C$ of goods may be defined by the requirement that:

$$(\forall s): C_s \supset C'.$$

Another concept here is that of *preference-consistency*, which makes it necessary that goods in C be ranked by each person in S, from those deemed most important for him to those which he feels are more 'dispensable'.

Preference-consistency is a property of the allocation of goods f, consisting of the fact that each set C_s contains an 'unbroken fragment' of goods, starting from the top, in the ranking of person s. Formally, if $>_s$ is the preference of person s in the set of goods, then the allocation f is preference-consistent, if:

$$(\forall s): c \in C_s \;\&\; c' >_s c \Longrightarrow c' \in C_s.$$

Finally, of basic importance for both theoretical analysis and for practice is the concept of *admissibility* of f. An allocation f is admissible, if there is no 'better' allocation f', such that it gives at least as many goods to anyone as f and anyhow more goods to some. Formally, f is admissible, if:

$$\sim (\exists f'): [(\forall s)\, C_s \subset C'_s \;\&\; (\exists s'): C_{s'} \neq C'_{s'}],$$

where C'_s are sets of goods enjoyed by s under f'.

The main problem for the theory of freedom considered is to determine a suitable class of *feasible* allocations f, and then look for various criteria, such as admissibility, etc. within this class.

5. Alienation and dynamics of social change

The present section will be devoted to an outline of the main ideas and results of the formal theory of alienation suggested by Nowakowska (1977, n.d.), according to which alienation is a state of being conscious of the fact that one is denied some goods which one expects and has the right to have because of the work one performs, or because of one's social status, etc.

Consider a fragment of the system (1), consisting of S, C, f and Π. For simplicity, let us assume that C contains only binary goods and, consequently, every allocation f (actual or hypothetical) assumes only the values 0 and 1.

Two basic additional concepts will be (a) the *admissibility* function $a(t, s, c)$, representing the degree to which giving goods c to person s at time t is admissible, and (b) the forces $F(s, f, f')$ and $G(s, f, f')$ which the person s is capable, given the present allocation f, of exerting respectively towards and against the change of the allocation f to an alternative f'.

The two main postulates assert the following:

1. Every $a(t, s, c)$, as a function of t, has at most one peak;
2. The change from f to f' will not occur, if the forces against it are stronger than those for it, i.e.

$$\sum_{s \in A} G(s,f,f') > \sum_{s \in B \cup C} F(s,f,f') \tag{4}$$

where A, B and C are respectively the sets of those persons s, who prefer f to f', who prefer f' to f, and who are indifferent between f and f'.

One can now define the admissibility of an allocation f, at time t, as follows:

$$A(t,f) = \min \{a(t,s,c) : f(s,c) = 1\}$$

Thus, the admissibility of the whole allocation is equal to the admissibility of the least admissible of its assignments of goods.

The first postulate implies that the function $A(t, f)$ also has the property of single-peakedness. This means that the admissibility of any allocation will eventually start diminishing.

Next, an allocation f is called *fair* (at time t), if $A(t, f) \geq A(t, f')$ for any alternative f' (i.e. f is the allocation with the highest possible admissibility). This definition covers to some extent the intuition of 'social justice'.

An allocation is called *stable*, if the inequality (4) holds for any alternative f'.

Since $A(t, f)$ will eventually begin to decline, there will appear at least one alternative f' which will be more fair than f. This leads to the following *dilemma*: if one wants to ensure fairness, one has to make changes; if one wants to preserve stability, one has to resign from fairness.

Any group of persons $M \subset A$ capable of ensuring the inequality:

$$\sum_{s \in M} G(s,f,f') > \sum_{s \notin M} F(s,f,f')$$

for some f' with $A(t,f') > A(t,f)$, i.e. capable of blocking the realization of a socially more fair alternative will be called a *monopole* with respect to the alternative f' (observe that since $M \subset A$, the last inequality implies the inequality (4)). The notion of enforcing monopole (as opposed to blocking monopole above) is defined similarly.

Since the forces F and G appearing in (4) are, in general, not known exactly, the problem of checking whether a group M is a monopole or not may be difficult. Generally, it appears that monopoles are fuzzy subsets of S.

Given these concepts, one can specify formal conditions for alienation of a person s.

Thus, suppose that actual allocation is f, and there exists an f' such that $f(s, c) = 0, f'(s, c) = 1$ for some goods c; that is, the person s does not have access to goods c under f, but would have such an access under f'.

If the following conditions are satisfied:

a. $a(t,s,c)$ is high and increasing;
b. $f' \pi_s f$ (i.e. s prefers f' to f);
c. $A(t,f') > A(t,f)$;
d. f' is blocked by some monopole M,

then one says that person s is *alienated* by the monopole M. Thus, alienation occurs if there is an alternative allocation f' which gives goods c to s, while he does not have these goods under f, and deserves them; moreover, this alternative f' is at the same time socially better than f, preferred by s, and blocked by a monopole.

The papers by Nowakowska (1977, n.d.) present a number of hypotheses about strategies of monopoles, and the effect of alienation on the tendencies to form counter-monopoles which try to induce a change in the allocation of goods. These hypotheses may therefore be treated as hypotheses about the dynamics which induce some special kind of social changes, namely those which consist of a transformation of allocation functions f.

Using the conditions (a) – (d) one may construct a measure of the strength of alienation.

Now, a person may be alienated with respect to various goods, by different monopoles, and one can therefore introduce such notions as the *scope* and *depth* of alienation, depending on the relative location of the alienating monopoles with respect to the person s.

When a large number of persons are alienated by the same monopole or monopoles and their communication network is sufficiently dense, there is a high probability that they will form a new social group, with its own goals, program of actions, etc., aimed primarily at a change reducing the alienation (i.e. a change of allocation). In this sense, alienation may produce also a social change in the form of a transformation of the structure $\mathscr{G}$, and the preferences (goal-structure) Π. Such social changes, as a rule, are preliminaries to major changes in allocations f.

One may therefore say that, given appropriate conditions, the phenomenon of alienation is a primary source of social changes, first in the 'consciousness domain', i.e. group structure $\mathscr{G}$ and preferences Π, and then (if the strength of the new group is sufficient, and the cost of change makes it feasible) also in the domain of allocation of goods.

6. A model of prosocial behaviour: adoption of group rules and reasons by individuals

In this section, the considerations will concern a fragment of system (1) consisting of one fixed social group G, with its goals induced by existing preference patterns, and consisting of individuals $s_1, \ldots, s_n$.

Contrary to the existing qualitative descriptions of the phenomenon of pro-, a- and antisociality, in which the tendency towards such types of behaviour is regarded as a personality trait, the present model (being the first formal theory of the phenomenon) attributes such behaviour to situational, social and psychological factors.

The starting point (see Nowakowska, 1977a) is the assumption that, in choosing a specific action, people tend to maximize the sum of the expected direct reward, and the 'indirect' reward, in the form of the evaluation of them by other members of the group, and consequently, acceptance or rejection by the group. These two types of reward are usually negatively related, i.e. increase of one of them brings about a decrease of the other.

More precisely, the i-th member of the group, s_i, will choose his action so as to maximize the quantity:

$$a_{ii}\Delta_c + \sum_{k \neq i} a_{ik}\Delta v\,(Q_{ki}), \tag{5}$$

where Δ_c is the change (positive or not) of individual satisfaction, due to gain or loss of goods c, $\Delta v\,(Q_{ki})$ is the change of evaluation of s_i by s_k, due to causing some events favourable or harmful to s_k, a_{ii} is the weight which s_i attaches to bringing satisfaction to himself, and a_{ik} is the weight which s_i attaches to the opinion of s_k.

Now, an action may be termed *prosocial* if it yields a negative value of Δ_c and a positive $\Delta v\,(Q_{ki})$ for all, or most, of indices k, and *antisocial* if the relation is opposite, i.e. if Δ_c is positive, and most (or all) $\Delta v\,(Q_{ki})$ are negative. An asocial action is such which yields positive Δ_c, while all $\Delta v\,(Q_{ki})$ are equal to zero.

The basic assumption concerns the value Q_{ki} (what s_k thinks about s_i), and $v\,(Q_{ki})$ (what s_i thinks that s_k thinks of him). It is namely assumed that Q_{ki} changes due to various actions of s_i, and s_k evaluates these actions from the point of view of the rules of the group. The changes are, in general, positive or negative, depending whether s_i's actions cause comfort or discomfort (harm) to s_k, except that when Q_{ki} gets below a rejection threshold, it may subsequently only decrease (i.e. after s_i did something 'unforgivable' from s_k's point of view, the latter rejects him, and his opinion of him may only get worse).

The function v is increasing, with the jump at the rejection threshold, so that generally, every person prefers to be valued highly by all, or most, members of the group, and has negative utility (feels punished) when rejected. The person's behaviour then depends on the character of the increase of the function v. If it becomes flat for values on the positive side (as Q_{ki} increases), the person attaches less and less weight to being accepted. If it becomes more steep as Q_{ki} increases, the person is 'acceptance-hungry'. On the other hand, if v becomes more flat as Q_{ki} decreases, the person has a bounded fear of rejection, while if it becomes more steep as Q_{ki} decreases, he has an unbounded fear of rejection.

This gives rise to a classification into four basic psychological types of persons by combining these two dichotomies of behaviour of the function v on the positive and the negative side (Figure 1).

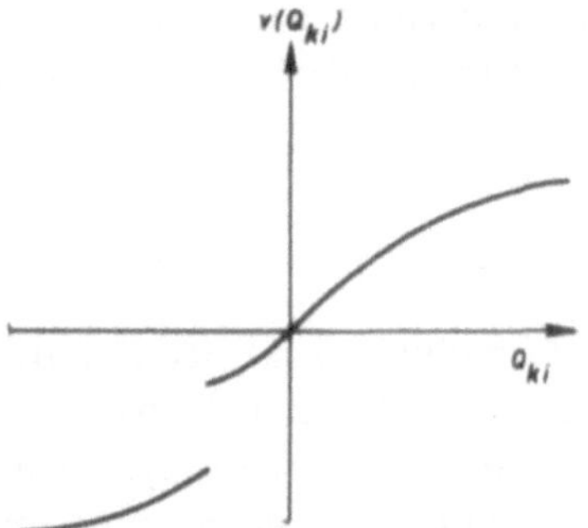

Type a. Limited need of acceptance; bounded fear of rejection.

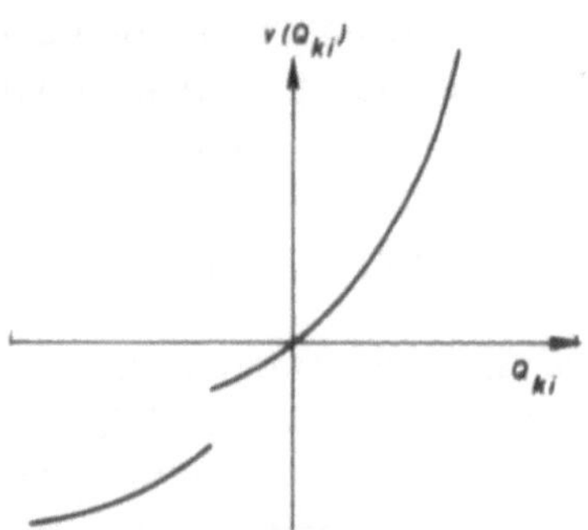

Type b. 'Acceptance-hungry'; bounded fear of rejection.

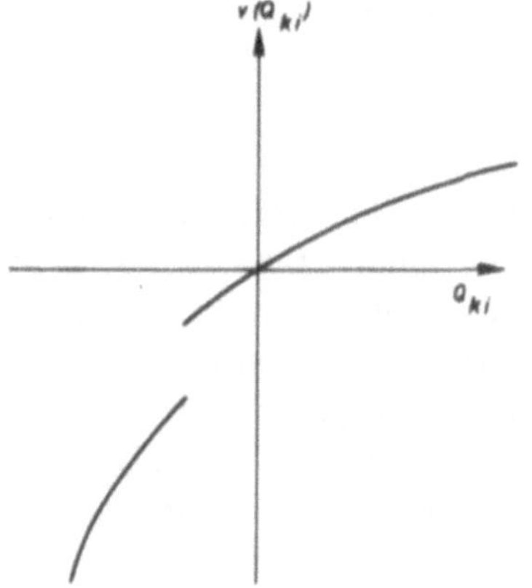

Type c. Limited need of acceptance; unbounded fear of rejection.

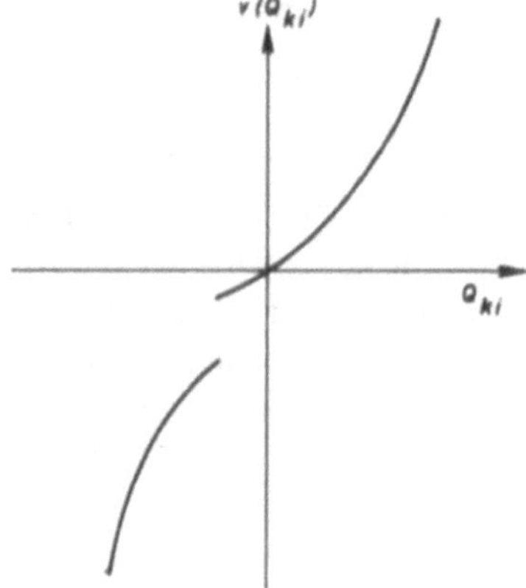

Type d. 'Acceptance-hungry'; unbounded fear of rejection.

Figure 1. Four basic psychological types of persons.

To use a simple example, in case *c*, if a person is highly accepted (see Figure 2), i.e. when Q_{ki} is far to the right, he is likely to behave in an antisocial way: lowering of Q_{ki} brings only a small decrease of $\Delta v\,(Q_{ki})$, as the function is flat in the acceptance region. Hence this decrease is easily counterbalanced by a positive reward Δ_c. On the other hand, such a type of person, if rejected, or threatened by rejection (Figure 3) is likely to behave in a prosocial way: lowering of Q_{ki} yields large negative $\Delta v\,(Q_{ki})$, hence not easily counterbalanced by reward Δ_c.

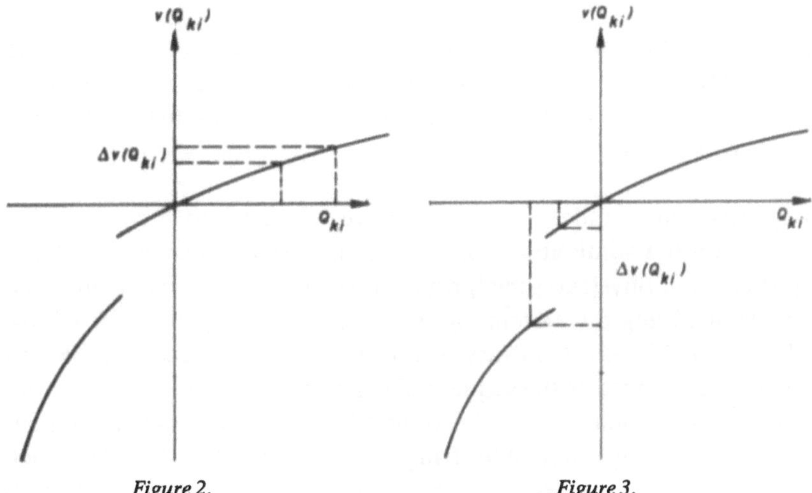

Figure 2. *Figure 3.*

This prediction takes into account only one value of Q_{ki}. In reality, as indicated in equation (5), there will be as many terms in the sum to be maximized as there are members of the group. The predictions can be made for all four types of persons, and they take on the following form:

Hypothesis 1.
Let a person's sensitivity to acceptance and rejection be limited (Type a). If he is differentially perceived, i.e. highly accepted by some and highly rejected by others, then his actions are likely to be asocial or antisocial. Otherwise, his actions are likely to be prosocial.

Hypothesis 2.
Let a person be dominated by the need of acceptance (while his fear of rejection is limited); this is Type b of Figure 1. If he is accepted by few, or merely tolerated, and rejected by many, his behaviour is likely to be asocial or antisocial. In the opposite case it is likely to be prosocial.

Hypothesis 3.
Let a person be dominated by fear of rejection, while his need of acceptance is bounded (Type c). If he is highly accepted by most, and rejected only by few, his behaviour is likely to be asocial or antisocial; otherwise, it is likely to be prosocial.

Hypothesis 4.
If a person has increasing sensitivity to both rejection and acceptance (Type d), he is likely to behave in a prosocial way, except perhaps in cases when he is neither rejected by many, nor accepted by many (i.e. when he is perceived indifferently by most).

In applying this model, one would have to take into account various constraints on the admissibility of actions other than those induced by the group rules (e.g. physical, social, psychological, organizational, etc.). This requires embedding the system into a wider theory of actions (see Nowakowska, 1973, 1973a). Contrary to the ideas of von Wright (1968), this theory of actions stresses the sequential character of actions, where various constraints make some strings of actions admissible and some inadmissible so that the class of all admissible strings of actions has the formal character of a language (set of admissible strings of words), with outcomes of actions playing the role of semantics.

Another problem is the knowledge of Q_{ki} by person s_i, that is, the knowledge of what others think about him. Such opinions are communicated verbally or non-verbally, and it is necessary to complement the system by a theory of such communication (see Nowakowska 1978).

Finally, it is worth remarking that the theory of prosocial behaviour, as outlined here, may be regarded (along with the theory of alienation) as the core of the theory of social change, suggesting numerous methods of sociotechniques useful in achieving behavioral changes.

7. A new approach to communication networks

In this section a model will be suggested for the study of the scope and speed of the dissemination of social change. The considerations will be based on an analysis of the communication network σ.

It is important to mention that the term 'communication' need not be treated literally. Formally, σ will be a binary relation in S, representing some types of social contacts, and it will be assumed that the objects which are disseminated in the society – such as news, innovations, diseases, opinions, ideas, etc. – are transmitted from one person to another if they are related by the relation σ.

The problem will be to study the proportion of persons whom the new idea eventually reaches, the speed of dissemination, etc.

There are basically two approaches possible here. One (very much explored, as the problem is one of the oldes in sociometry and has already a long research tradition), is to make some assumptions about the relation σ, and then try to deduce the properties of interest from these assumptions. Such an approach is reasonable for small groups. However, for a society consisting of a large number of individuals (millions, if one considers social groups such as a nation, the inhabitants of a town, etc.), such an approach appears impossible. Thus, an alternative is to assume that the relation σ is random and to analyse the probabilities of various events, especially those which have a probability close to 1 (such events are of primary interest, since they allow us to infer that analogous events must occur in the real society, regardless of the specific form of its relation σ).

To proceed formally, it will be more convenient to denote the fact that the elements are related through the relation σ by an arrow: thus, $s \to t$ means that there is relation between s and t (but not necessarily t and s).

One can now define the relations $\underset{n}{\to}$ as follows:

a. $s \underset{1}{\to} t$ *if* $s \to t$

b. $s \underset{n}{\to} t$ if $(\exists x): s \underset{n-1}{\to} x$ and $x \underset{1}{\to} t$.

Finally, a double arrow will indicate the sum of all relations $\underset{n}{\to}$, i.e. the transitive closure of $\to$:

$$s \Rightarrow t \text{ if } (\exists n): s \underset{n}{\to} t.$$

Let now s be fixed, and consider the sets:

$$A(s) = \{t: s \Rightarrow t\}$$

and

$$B(s) = \{t: t \Rightarrow s\}.$$

Thus, if the relation $\to$ is represented in the form of a directed graph, with nodes at the points $s \in S$ and edges corresponding to pairs connected by the relation $\to$, then $A(s)$ is the set of all points which may be reached from s if one proceeds along the arrows, and $B(s)$ is the set of elements which can be reached from s by going counter to the arrows.

Moreover, if $D \subset S$, then:

$$A(D) = \bigcup_{s \in D} A(s)$$

and

$$B(D) = \bigcup_{s \in D} B(s)$$

are the set of all points which may be reached from any of the nodes in D by proceeding respectively along and contrary to the arrows.

Now, if the relation $\rightarrow$ is random, then the sets $A(D)$ and $B(D)$ are also random. One of the interesting questions is: suppose that the set D contains k elements, and that the set S contains n elements. Given the average number of edges leaving a given node to be q, what is the distribution of the size of the sets $A(D)$ and $B(D)$, and in particular, what is the probability that $A(D) = S$?

For a possible application, imagine that D is the set of persons who originate some new idea, and that this idea spreads across the society, say, with the direction of arrows. Then $A(D)$ is the set of persons who will eventually be 'infected' with the idea.

One can conjecture here that there will exist a *density threshold*; this conjecture may be formulated as follows. For a fixed n and k (sizes of S and D), and the average number of edges per node q (so that there are nq edges altogether), let:

$$P_{n,k,q}(|A(D)| \geq \alpha n)$$

be the probability that the size of the set $A(D)$ will exceed αn $(0 < \alpha \leq 1)$, i.e. that the 'infection' will cover the fraction α of the society.

Hypothesis 5.
For sufficiently large n, fixed k and α, there exists a threshold in q, i.e. $P_{n,k,q}(|A(D)| \geqq \alpha n)$ is close to 0 if q is less than this threshold, and close to 1 if q exceeds this threshold.

Hypothesis 6.
For sufficiently large n, fixed q and α, there exists a threshold in k, such that $P_{n,k,q}(|A(D)| \geqq \alpha n)$ is close to 0 if k is below the threshold, and close to 1 otherwise.

The first of these hypotheses predicts essential qualitative changes in the scope and spread of the idea when the density of relations (frequency of contacts, 'tightness' of the society, etc.) exceeds a certain limit. The second hypothesis predicts the same phenomenon under the change of the size of the initial set.

If these hypotheses are true, they would have some very interesting social implications concerning the optimal choice of network density and also the optimal choice of the size of a group which is to effectively spread its ideas across a society.

The suggested approach also offers numerous other possibilities. To mention just one of them, suppose that one wants to study resistance to accepting new ideas before passing them on (this may be interpreted, for instance, as ideological resistance, etc.). This may be attained by assuming simply that information (idea, etc.) is accepted by a person only if he receives it from at least m sources, so that m is a measure of his resistance. Thus, the spreading proceeds as before except that it leaves a given node only if there are m arrows leading to it, each of these arrows originating again from a node, to which there are at least m arrows, and so on. Here also one may expect some threshold effects, under the change of 'resistance' expressed by the number m, on the probability that a given fraction α of the society will eventually be 'infected'.

8. Some of the further perspectives

One of the principal lines of research, which will be briefly sketched here, would consist of considering the system (1) together with an appropriate action system built along the lines suggested in Nowakowska (1973). Consider namely a social group $G \in \mathcal{G}$ consisting of $s_1, \ldots, s_n$.

As already stated, the goals for each person, and the goals of the group as a whole, can be expressed in terms of preferences over the set of allocations of goods in S. These goals are, of course, structured in some way, i.e. achievement of some goals may facilitate achieving other goals, etc. This is due to the fact that achieving of a goal specified, say, in the form of a new allocation of goods f, yields new powers to various members of the group, so that they may find it easier to change f into some other allocation f', and so on.

In addition, the goals (preferential structures) of social groups may be related in some way across groups. The basic types of relations here are *concordance*, *orthogonality*, and *opposition*. The first and third of these relations require no comments as they simply mean an agreement and disagreement of preferential orderings, while orthogonality means that whenever an alternative is strictly preferred to another by one group then these two alternatives are indifferent from the point of view of the other group. There is no need to stress the importance of these notions for any theory of coalitions and conflicts between social groups.

Returning to the case of a single group, its goal may therefore be formally identified with a *class of sequences of allocations* $f, f', f'', \ldots$. Each allocation in such a sequence may be regarded as a conjunction of various conditions, stating that such and such goods are to be allocated to such and such persons at a given stage of pursuit of the goal.

Any such class of sequences may be represented in the form of a 'goal-tree', consecutive branches corresponding to the terms of sequences.

To bring about such changes as specified by the goal, i.e. to achieve successive transitions to f, then to f', then to f'', ... as specified by the goal, the group as a whole must plan and perform some actions. Such a plan, covering all possibilities, i.e. specifying the actions in each node of the tree of the goal, is called a *strategy*.

Generally, with each person $s \in G$ one may associate his action repertoire, say $U(s)$. The actions in various sets $U(s)$ are, as a rule, mutually related – in the sense that performing some actions from $U(s)$ may inhibit the possibilities of performing some other actions from $U(s')$. Such constraints on actions are induced by various factors, among them by the set R of rules accepted by the group. Moreover, as the set R is structured, various constraints on actions have a different 'degree of tightness', i.e. breaking some of these rules is considered 'worse', from the point of view of the group, than breaking others. These features were not considered in the section on prosocial behaviour, where it was simply assumed that each member of the group judges the actions of others according to the rules, and assigns to them some aggregated index Q_{ki}. Of course, a more subtle theory would have to also consider the ways by which a person attains such a judgment.

Generally, actions of a group may be divided into three broad categories. Two of them refer to actions aimed at attaining an allocation from a set specified by the goal-tree. Such actions may, in turn, be divided into direct and indirect, where the latter differ from the first in that they refer rather to the 'ideological' domain, by providing, for instance, the justifications, reasons, etc. for the necessity of a given allocation of goods. This type of actions consists, therefore, of providing and disseminating the premises for the necessity of a given change of allocation of goods, its admissibility, etc., or the premises for preserving the present allocation.

The third type of actions of the group may be called internal. The point is that when a group as a whole receives a certain amount of goods, as specified by its goal, the problem arises of allocating these goods within the group. Formally, the (partial) goal of the group may be to bring about any allocation which provides the total amount K of goods c, i.e. any allocation which satisfies the condition:

$$\sum_{s \in G} f(s, c) = K$$

(plus a number of other constraints). Denoting the class of allocations which meet the above conditions by $F_{K,c}$, the problem is to choose a particular allocation in this class. This depends, of course, on the internal structure of the group, and the forces which operate within it, the powers of various members, and so on.

9. Some hypotheses

There is no need to point out that this paper gives only a very brief sketch of a proposed theory of social change, with many details to be filled in and worked out, and a number of aspects of the phenomenon to be included in addition to those already embedded in the model. Clearly, such a task is beyond the scope of a short paper, and therefore the aim here was to outline the basic ideas and formal constructions rather than to provide a complete description.

To illustrate, however, the potential applicability and richness of the approach, some hypotheses will be formulated in addition to those given in the preceding sections.

Firstly, a social change was defined as a 'substantial' change in any of the variables appearing in (1). Whether a given change is accepted (or perceived) as substantial, hence whether it might be classified by a given individual as a social change, depends on many factors, mainly on the person's position in S, and his level of alienation. We have namely:

Hypothesis 7.
Any person has a *threshold*, above which he tends to classify a given change as substantial. This threshold, in general, is:
a. Different for different types of change (variables in system (1));
b. Higher for changes which affect positively the judging person, and lower if they affect him negatively;
c. In both cases, negatively related to the alienation level of the person.

Another important aspect of the social change is connected with the concepts sketched briefly in the preceding section. The point here is that the theory based on system (1) covers what may be termed 'total' social changes along one or more of the dimensions specified in (1). One can also consider 'local' social changes, restricted to one or more of the groups, and consisting of the changes of the strategies; changes of goals, as involving the preferential structures, changes of rules, as involving sets R, and changes of structures of the groups themselves, as involving $\mathscr{G}$, would be classified as 'total' changes even if they are restricted to one group only, and leave invariant the allocations, rules, etc. outside a given group.

The change of strategy means here a change in the stress on the allocation of efforts by a group among the three domains of its activity: ideological (A_1), factual (A_2), and internal (A_3). Here one may formulate the following:

Hypothesis 8.
During the time preceding and immediately following a social change in the form of a transition to a new allocation of goods f, the group activities are concentrated at first mostly on activities of type A_1, then on activities of type A_2, and then, in the period immediately preceding the transition, and following it, on activities of types A_3 and A_1.

Hypothesis 9.
As the admissibility of the actual allocation decreases (as it must, according to the postulates of Section 4), the groups interested in preserving it will concentrate mainly on activities of the types A_1 and A_3, while the groups interested in changing it will concentrate mainly on activities of the types A_2 and A_1.

Hypothesis 10.
The effectiveness of activity of the type A_1 depends primarily on the properties of the network σ and increases with the increase of the value q, the average number of connections per node.

Hypothesis 11.
The increase of intensity of activity of the type A_1 (ideological) by two or more groups with opposing preference patterns Π leads to a decrease of fuzziness in the group structure $\mathcal{G}$ ('polarization of the society').

Hypothesis 12.
Major changes in the structure and/or content of the sets of rules R associated with various groups are usually followed by major changes in the group structure $\mathcal{G}$ itself, by leading to the appearance of new social groups.

As already mentioned, the main driving forces behind social changes are induced by alienation of members of various groups. Thus, the hypotheses about alienation and strategies of monopoles (see Nowakowska, 1977) are relevant for the proposed theory of social change. In particular, one should mention here the following hypotheses:

Hypothesis 13.
A blocking monopole, hence a monopole interested in *preventing* a social change adverse to its interests, will tend to support other social changes, in particular those which lead to an increase of the total admissibility of allocations, hence also leading to a decrease of level of alienation.

Hypothesis 14.
A social change in the form of an appearance of a new group structure

$\mathscr{G}$, through the creation of a counter-monopole, is more likely in cases when the level of alienation is high, and its variance is small, than in the opposite cases.

Finally, the following hypothesis is relevant for the prediction of dynamics of monopoles, hence also the dynamics of the group structure $\mathscr{G}$.

Hypothesis 15.
If $f(t)$ is the probability that the person's duration of participation in a monopole is exactly t, and $F(t)$ is the probability that it is t or less, then the ratio $f(t)/(1-F(t))$ is an increasing function of t.

This last hypothesis, asserting the 'aging property' of the distribution $f(t)$ of participation in a monopole is justified by the intuition according to which the longer a person is in a monopole, the more chances that he is satisfied with the goods he received, and therefore the more chances he will attempt to join another monopole.

The preceding hypotheses concerned the role of alienation in inducing social change. In connection with this, one can also state the following hypotheses of a 'negative' character.

Hypothesis 16.
A social change is less likely to occur if the alienated groups:
1. receive some 'goods-substitutes', as long as they are approved as valuable, or
2. the group activity is directed towards some 'action-substitutes', or
3. the groups' present goods allocation is threatened.

Hypothesis 17.
If the group is under negative information pressure organized by competing groups, it may decrease the likelihood of real changes by making apparent changes (e.g. through semantically equivalent phrasing of programs, reasons and rules).

Hypothesis 18.
The tighter a group is organized, and the more such a group approves of its reasons and program the more resistant it will be to new ideas, and the less prone to change.

10. Conclusions and possible extensions

The theory presented here, because of space limitations, was only sketched in rough outline. The main problem, that of modelling the behaviour of a large system and the dynamics of social change, was dealt with by constructing some submodels covering the most important socioeconomic and sociopsychological mechanisms. The set of possible hypotheses is far from exhaustive, even for an abbreviated version of the theory. It seems, however, that the theory outlined adequately shows the cognitive possibilities of the model.

To summarize the main points of the paper: its basis is a formal scheme for describing the structure of the society, consisting of the following seven primitives: the set of individuals S; the class of various (possible overlapping) social groups; the set of goods; their distribution among members of S; individual preferences of members of the society among the distributions of goods; sets of rules operating within social groups and constraining their actions; and finally, the communication network. Within this formal setup, one can analyse various social phenomena. Thus, one may use the scheme to build a formal theory of social freedom by considering a special category of goods, such as voting rights, privileges, etc. Next, one may construct a dynamic theory of structural change of the society, formally explicating the phenomena of monopolization of power and alienation of various members of the society.

Analysis of the relationships between a group and its members leads to a new decision model allowing prediction of prosocial or antisocial behaviour. Finally, analysis of social communication networks leads to various conjectures about the existence of a threshold density of such networks, above which a new idea has a high probability of spreading across a substantial part of the society.

Space limitations did not allow a demonstration here of the analysis of informational fights between groups, the structure and dynamics of their informational microparadigms, the diffusion of information to other groups, and the energy invested by a given group to create its persistent self-image, etc.

The paper ends with the formulation of a number of testable hypotheses about the particular aspects of social changes in the paper.

One of the important subsystems which was omitted in the paper concerns the set of possible rules constraining actions of members of particular groups. This subsystem constitutes, in fact, a rich self-contained theory of actions, presented in the book by Nowakowska (1973), allowing a formal explication and characterization by theorems of such aspects as goal structure, attainability of goals, praxiological, economical and ethical valuations of strings of actions, consistency between verbal and nonverbal behaviour, structure of human motivation and its linguistic representation, and both interpersonal and intrapersonal conflicts. It is worth while to point out that this theory appeared very fruitful in applications, especially to the problems of communication and dialogues, and foundations of semiotics (see Nowakowska 1976, 1977, 1978), generating new systems with interesting properties to describe these phenomena.

From the point of view of the fashionable new problems of consiousness, the model of prosocial behaviour shows how the judgments of what someone thinks others think about him influences his behaviour. Such judgments are one of the examples of approximate reasoning, that is, of inference drawn from utterances in the natural language, and from nonverbal cues. In the book quoted above (Nowakowska 1973), approximate reasoning was analysed, using the name 'motivational calculus', for a class of motivational functors. The central concept there was that of semantic implication, this being a relationship between sentences in modal frames. Its definition, based on the concept of semantic admissibility, weakens the material and strict implications. Moreover, it is also possible to define the strength of semantic implication through some linguistic variables. Motivational calculus is a set of transformation rules for sentences, proved to be consistent by a set theoretical model.

In this short sketch it was not even possible to mention such other concepts as motivational (cognitive) space, its structure, and sorting properties in all classes of situations in which one has to judge, explain or justify the planned or past actions. The complementary theories mentioned above allow one to deepen some of the subsystems of the presented theory of social change that was presented.

References

Arrow, K. J., *Social choice and individual values*, New York: Wiley, 1963.

Nowakowska, M., *Language of motivation and language of actions*, The Hague: Mouton, 1973.

Nowakowska, M., 'A formal theory of actions.' *Behavioral Science* 18, 1973(a).

Nowakowska, M., 'Monopolization and alienation in science: a formal approach.' *Behavioral Science* 22, 1977.

Nowakowska, M., 'Towards a formal theory of freedom.' *Management Science* 1977 (in press).

Nowakowska, M., 'Prosocial behavior: a decision model.' *Polish Psychological Bulletin* 8 (3), 1977(a).

Nowakowska, M., 'Verbal and nonverbal communication as a multidimensional language' in T. Borbé (ed.) *Proc. Second Vienna Symposium on Semiotics.* (in press), 1978.

Nowakowska, M., 'Alienation: a formal theory' n.d. in R. Felix Geyer and David R. Schweitzer (eds.): forthcoming publication, containing a selection of papers delivered at meetings of Ad Hoc Group on Alienation Theory and Research, Uppsala, 1978.

Nowakowska, M., 'Object and its verbal copy: towards a formal foundation of semiotics. In T. Borbé (ed.) *Proc. Third Vienna Symposium on Semiotics*, (in press).

Wright, G. H. von, *An essay in deontic logic and the general theory of actions*, Amsterdam: North Holland, 1968.

Zadeh, L. A., 'Fuzzy sets.' *Information and Control* 8, 1965.

Are societies Turing machines? Some implications of the cyclical majority problem, an NP complete problem, for cybernetic models of social systems

Don M. M. Booker

1. Cybernetic models of social systems

The paradigms of cybernetic models of social systems are frequently finite automata. Such models, implicitly or explicitly, require a decision procedure for multi-attribute value aggregation. This decision procedure requires either a hierarchical ordering of sub- and supra-systems, or is reduced to the cyclical majority problem. Many well-known applications of cybernetic concepts to the analysis of social systems have been aimed at constructing formal models of society and using these models to examine processes which could be described by finite automata[1]. The outstanding work of Buckley[2], Parsons[3] and Etzioni[4] in sociology; of Deutsch[5] and Easton[6] in political science; and of Forrester[7], D. H. Meadows, D. L. Meadows, Randers and Behrens[8], and Mesarovic and Pestel[9] in social systems simulation exemplify this approach. Simulations of political processes in Shaffer[10], Pool[11], and Klausner[12] typify cybernetic models expressed as implicit theory embodied in computer programs (as noted by Browning)[13], as well as showing the behavior of the explicit processes which the programs model.

Laszlo[14] typifies and summarizes these paradigms with a definition of social systems or human societies as the joint function ('social natural system') of the independent variables: wholeness, adaptability, self-organization, and inter-systems and intra-systems hierarchy.[15]

1.1. Complexity and hierarchical structure

Such cybernetic models of social systems require a functional description of decision processes in the society and the resultant control processes of the society.

Simon suggests that:

'hierarchy is the adaptive form for finite intelligence to assume in the face of complexity.... The near universality of hierarchy in the composition of complex systems suggests that there is something fundamental in this structural principle that goes beyond the peculiarities of human organization.'[16]

Both self-organization and efficiency in the complexity of internal communications and control tend to encourage hierarchical structures.

Pattee notes:

'increasing complexity of organization is always accompanied by new levels of hierarchical controls.... As systems grow in size and complexity they reach a limit where a new level of hierarchical control is necessary if the system is to function realiably.'[17]

1.2. Criterion functions and hierarchical structure

In discussing the application of cybernetic models to management decision, Simon gives a 'general recipe' for their use: '(1) Construct a *mathematical model*... (2) Define the *criterion function*... (3) Obtain *empirical estimates* of the numerical parameters in the model. (4) Carry through the mathematical process which... maximizes the criterion function.'[18] Simon also emphasizes that:

'certain conditions must be satisfied in order to apply this recipe to a class of decision problems. First it must be possible to define mathematical variables that represent the important aspects of the situation. In particular, a quantitative criterion function must be defined.'[19]

Our interest in the cyclical majority problem focuses upon the interaction between the construction of a mathematical model, in particular its implicit or explicit structure, and the *criterion* function. All decision systems require some criterion function, either as an objective function or imbedded in the structure of the model itself. If the criterion function is imbedded in the model itself, it is frequently in the form of a hierarchical structure. This hierarchical structure may reflect the environment being modeled, or may be due to the necessity to impose tractable order on a complex model or computer program.

For example, much of the current work in large and complex computer program design utilizing structured design methodologies[20] is aimed at reliable hierarchical partitioning of complex programs. Simon also notes:

'whenever highly complex programs have been written... they have always turned out to have a clear-cut hierarchical structure... Moreover, in some general sense, the higher level programs control or govern the behavior of the lower level programs, so that we find among these programs relations of authority among routines that are not dissimilar to those we are familiar with in human organizations.'[21]

The most important effect of the pervasiveness and likelihood of hierarchical structures in cybernetic models of social systems which we wish to emphasize is their *secondary function as an implicit criterion function*. This effect is twofold. If we are not explicit in our definition of a criterion function we may inadvertantly impose one by the hierarchical structure of our model; the opposite error may also occur. Even though the structure appears hierarchical, and therefore transitive, if it involves a decision procedure that requires the aggregation of criterion functions, or value outputs from subsystems, the hierarchical structure alone will not guarantee a transitive value ordering if the subsystem outputs are rank orderings, which are individually transitive but not reducible to a common measure.

This process is also illustrated in large, complex computer programs. Even though the program is formally structured as a hierarchy of control, the activation of parallel processes attempting to utilize the same set of resources in sequence may lead to an interlock problem.[22] This problem occurs where one activity awaits the release of a resource by another activity which is, in turn, awaiting the release of a second resource by the first activity. Clearly, neither activity can proceed and they remain locked in a 'deadly embrace'. Formally each individual activity exhibits a transitive ordering of priorities for resources, but aggregation results in a non-transitive sum over the relation 'waits.' The use of such programming design methods as parallel processes[23], coroutines[24], and ring structures[25] in complex data management systems, requires control techniques beyond simple hierarchical subroutine calls to coordinate their behavior on a horizontal execution level, (such interprogram control structures require an additional formal rule or order for activation which infuses a transitive ranking) in addition to the vertical hierarchical order supplied by their invocation and linkage structures.

2. The cyclical majority problem

Any decision structure entails an assumption defining the aggregation of value, or the imposition of some scale of value, albeit 'hidden,' on the structure of the decision process. If we restrict this scale to single rank order measures output by individual subsystems, or input from the environment, we may pose the problem in a general form. The aggregation of individual, or subsystem, preference functions that are simple rank order into a group or system decision function, without recourse to the use of an external, or imposed, measure provides a formulation which reduces to the cyclical majority problem.

2.1. History of the cyclical majority problem

The cyclical majority problem was mentioned by Condorcet in the eighteenth century and is also frequently referred to as the Condorcet effect. It was also independently discovered by Borda in the eighteenth century. It was later commented upon by Dodgson (Lewis Carroll), who originated the term 'cyclical majority' which we will use to describe the problem. It was most recently 'rediscovered' by Arrow[26], and is frequently referred to in contemporary discussions as 'the Arrow paradox.' Arrow and Riker[27] provide a thorough discussion of the history of the problem.

Guilbaud[28] provided the first hint at an analytical solution to the problem. Niemi and Weisberg[29], Garman and Kamien[30], and Roberts[31] provide a full analytical treatment. Calculations and simulations of the problem for small (less than 40) values of judges and choices have been done by Campbell and Tullock[32], Klahr[33], and Pomeranz and Weil[34]. More recently, interest has been focused on the problem of 'invisible dictators' (an aspect of the problem we also emphasize as often implicit in hierarchical structures) by Kirman and Sondermann[35], and Hansson[36]. Fishburn[37] and Hansson[38] have also examined the problem for the case of an infinite number of voters.

2.2. A formal statement of the cyclical majority problem

This unresolved combinatorial problem has significant normative implications which have concerned economists and political scientists for some time. We shall examine the problem in a form posed by Pomeranz and Weil[39]. We wish to determine the likelihood of a cyclical majority occurring as the number of issues, and the number of judges, becomes large (or as the system size and complexity increase.) We choose this form since it may also be expressed as an integer programming problem. Karp[40] has shown that the 0/1 integer programming problem falls into the class of NP complete problems, therefore we will show the cyclical majority problem is also an NP complete problem.

We may state the cyclical majority decision problem formally as:

The *decision problem* requires:

- A set of n choices (or objects) to be ranked in a preference ordering $n_1Rn_2R\ldots Rn_n$.
- A set of m judges.

Subject to:

- The assumption of an odd number, m, of judges.
- The assumption that each judge is equally likely to have any one of the $n!$ possible preference orderings as his preference ordering over the n choices.
- The number of choices, n, is at least 1 greater than the number of judges, m.

The *decision procedure* is a simple summation:

- A *group decision* is reached by summing the rankings of all judges over each issue, over all issues.
- A group preference ordering or decision in which any one of the n choices is ranked above all other choices by more than $m/2$ judges will be termed a *majority decision*.
- If there is no majority decision, a *cyclical majority* is said to have occurred.
- The *cyclical majority problem* involves determining the likelihood of a cyclical majority resulting from some particular group decision as m, the number of judges, and n, the number of choices, both become very large, but remain finite.

We define:

$\mathbf{J}(m,n)$: An individual judge's binary choice matrix $(n \times n)$ for each judge such that:
$a_{ij}=1$ if the column choice is preferred to the row choice,
$a_{ij}=0$ otherwise.

For example:

	a	b	c	d
a	0	1	1	1
b	0	0	1	1
c	0	0	0	1
d	0	0	0	0

Indicates:
(*R*:: 'is preferred to')
d *R* c *R* b *R* a
a *R* 0

$\mathbf{G}(m, n)$: A group choice matrix, $n \times n$, for all m judges

$$\mathbf{G}(m, n) = \sum_{1}^{m} \mathbf{J}(m, n)$$

such that:
- Any row, $\mathbf{r}_n$, of **G**, with all entries less than $m/2$, is defined as the majority choice.
- If all rows, **r**, of **G**, each have at least one entry greater than $m/2$, a cyclical majority is said to have occurred.

2.3. Arrow's paradox

Arrow's formulation of this problem specified four axioms and an Impossibility Theorem. Given at least two judges and three alternatives, and a set of all preference orders for the judges, over the alternatives, the Impossibility Theorem asserts there is no 'social welfare function' (or majority decision, in our terms) which satisfies all four axioms. The axioms all appear to be intuitively necessary for any democratic process of social decision. They specify various reasonable goals for such a decision process in a precise logical form. Axiom 1 requires a positive association of social and individual values; axiom 2 requires the independence of irrelevant alternatives; axiom 3 requires citizens' sovereignty; and axiom 4, non-dictatorship.

2.4. Probabilistic models of the cyclical majority problem

Extensive previous work has focused on stating and solving the problem in a probabilistic form. Niemi and Weisberg state, 'the probability of no majority winner with m individuals and n alternatives, to be denoted by $\mathrm{P}(m, n)$, is the complement of the sum of the probabilities that each alternative wins.'[41] They have estimated the probability of a cyclical majority for n up to 40, m up to 40. Unfortunately, as Garman and Kamien note, 'a closed expression for Θ (n) (P(m, n) in Niemi and Weisberg's notation) for larger n does not exist so far as we know.'[42] Thus, for the present, we have no solution beyond an (m, n) of 50. However, the likelihood of a cyclical majority appears to increase as n and m become large.

2.5. The invisible dictator: structure or finitude?

Extrapolating the probabilistic simulation results of Pomeranz and Weil would indicate that a cyclical majority approaches certainty as n and m become large. However, Fishburn[43] has shown that Arrow's Impossibility Theorem does not hold for the case of an infinite number of voters.

Hansson helps to clarify this seeming anomaly:

'...it seems as if the importance of the concept "invisible dictator" is impossible to determine in general, but varies to a very high degree with the naturalness of the topologies of particular applications. In some cases, as e.g. the alternatives are functions over time and the "voters" points on the time axis, it is of great significance, but in others, among them those with unstructured voter sets, it is more like a terminological trick.'[44]

Which unfortunately still leaves the problem unresolved for the finite, but very large, case.

The 'invisible dictator' problem focuses on the difficulty of satisfying axioms 3 and 4. Other efforts have focused on relaxing other axioms.[45] The 'invisible dictator' may take the form of the hierarchical structure of the entire model in which the majority decision problem is embedded, thus implicitly rather than explicitly violating Arrow's 4th axiom.[46]

3. Computational complexity and NP complete problems

In order to consider the limits on the finite solution of the cyclical majority problem it is necessary to introduce some arguments from automata and complexity theory involving Turing machines.[47] At this point we are only concerned with a Turing machine (TM) as a device for the recognition of formal languages. (Later we shall return to its more general use as a model of social systems.)

Following Weide's[48] excellent survey of computational complexity, we may define the class P of problems solvable in polynomial time as:

'...the set of languages which are recognized by some deterministic TM that always halts in a number of steps which is bounded by a fixed polynomial in the length of the input (i.e. 'polynomial time'). Similarly the class NP (for "Nondeterministic Polynomial") is the set of languages which are recognized by some *non*deterministic TM in polynomial time. A nondeterministic TM operates in polynomial time if all sequences of choices of moves are of polynomial bounded length; a string is accepted by such a machine if there exists any such sequence of steps which leads to an accepting state.[49]

It is currently an open question in complexity theory whether P = NP, but experience supports the conjecture that P ≠ NP, even though 'if there is a polynomial time deterministic algorithm for *any* [my emphasis] NP complete problem then P = NP.'[50]

Weide succinctly describes the critical argument delimiting the class of 'NP complete' problems:

'The key to the argument that P ≠ NP is a remarkable theorem by Cook stating that every problem in NP can be polynomially reduced to Boolean satisfiability. This problem is very simply stated: Is there an assignment of truth values to the literals of a Boolean expression which makes the expression true? This means that every problem which can be solved in polynomial time on a nondeterministic TM can also be solved by subjecting the input string to a transformation (done deterministically in polynomial time) that converts it to an instance of satisfiability, and then solving the resulting satisfiability problem. Many other problems have subsequently been shown to have the same property. A problem such as satisfiability is called "NP complete".'[51]

3.1. NP complete formulation of the cyclical majority problem

If we express the cyclical majority problem formally as described above, then it may be seen to be a case of Boolean satisfiability. We have a set of j, $n \times n$ matrices of j judges' binary choices over n alternatives, which is equivalent to a string of Boolean variables $j \times n^2$ in length. We wish to assign values to these variables such that some true cyclical majority expression can be found for the string, for all judges over all alternatives as the number of judges and the number of alternatives increases finitely without limit.

Karp[52] has applied Cook's method to a large class of problems and shown that many optimatization and graph problems are reducible NP complete problems. These problems include 0/1 integer programming, the traveling salesman problem, the knapsack problem, and graph coloring. If any one of these problems is solvable in polynomial time then all of them are. These results suggest that alternatively, we might also formulate the cyclical majority problem as a 0/1 integer programming problem. This alternative formulation is even more convincing of the 'hardness' of the cyclical majority problem than a satisfiability formulation, since a very large number of algorithms and solution methods exists for this class of optimization problems.

'This fact forms the basis for believing (even if one cannot prove) that P ≠ NP, since none of the hundreds of algorithms for the scores of problems that are NP complete was in polynomial time. If any of these problems could be solved quickly, all of them could be; the fact that so far none of them can be is a convincing argument (although not a proof) that they never will be.'[53]

3.2. Practical and theoretical computation limits

We face both theoretical and practical, or implementation level, constraints on the modeling of social systems. If the cyclical majority were not an NP complete problem we might expect to find a fast or efficient computational algorithm telling us whether, as the number of judges and the number of choices increase, there exists any dominant majority decision function; if any such function exists, it might represent a negligibly small frequency of possible majority decisions. The additional practical difficulty of computing solutions to similar problems with currently available techniques is also discouraging but not unexpected.

In addition, the execution of programs to solve some linear programming problems on digital computers exhibit cycling when they begin to approach the size or complexity of problems such as those in which we are interested in the cyclical majority problem. In these cases, rather than considering the ill conditioned behavior of the model to be an artifact of the limitations of the hardware or software used, it may be indicative of a more general problem which had previously been hidden by actual artifacts which represented actually feasible solutions as unfeasible because, as noted by Kotiah and Steinberg, 'round off errors in the computations perturb the problem sufficiently to prevent cycling.'[54] This implies that the value of recourse to techniques of computer simulation and the computational algorithms provided for the solution of various optimization problems necessary for the modeling of significant social problems may be restricted by its cost in time, as well as limitations on execution time accuracy.

If we reduce the cyclical majority problem to either a Boolean satisfiability problem or an 0/1 integer programming problem, it is NP complete and equivalently reducible cybernetic models of social systems are also NP complete hard problems. Such problems do not currently appear to be solvable in polynomial time, and in fact frequently show a solution time which increases exponentially with the number of alternatives considered. Even if the process being modeled has a more constrained description, so long as we must use a rank order measure and construct a group decision function such as we have described above, we will be constrained by the NP complete nature of the problem. This may be the case even when the 'group' decision models the aggregation of values over a multi-attribute value space by an 'individual' decision maker.[55]

The inclusion of the cyclical majority problem in the class of NP complete problems carries with it several critical implications for the cybernetic modeling of social systems. The practical implication of the 'hardness', or difficulty, of the solution (the extreme cost in computational time and the resulting difficulty of the calculation of solutions to interesting problems in this class) indicates the need for restraint in practical expectations.

4. Empirical considerations: modifying the equally likely assumption

The identification of the cyclical majority problem as an NP complete problem provides an explanation for its continued resistance to earlier attempts at 'solution.' Many earlier efforts focused on detailed analysis of the logic of the problem, in essence attempting to solve it by hand as a Boolean satisfiability problem.[56] These approaches generally resulted in the conclusion that one of Arrow's axioms must be relaxed in order to modify his Impossibility Theorem. This is intuitively appealing since Arrow's axioms and his Impossibility Theorem seem to contradict the fundamental myths underlying democratic decision processes and ideologies. This apparent paradox provides a motivation for attacking the formal logic of the cyclical majority problem itself. In general, the social systems analyst, to say nothing of the computer he uses, is extremely uncomfortable with paradoxical results. This is particularly true when we 'know' that social processes we are attempting to model do, in fact, reach decisions. We feel, naturally enough, that our model should be able to replicate the process. Although simulations indicate an increasing likelihood of a cyclical majority as the number of judges and the number of choices increases, it has been suggested that actual cases of the cyclical majority are rare.[57]

One source of an explanation for this apparent rarity lies in the theoretical assumption that all *n* choice events are 'equally likely.' That is, that all *n* events are 'equally likely' to be chosen as most preferred, by any one of the *m* judges. In most actual decision situations the 'equally likely' condition seems to be 'unlikely' for psychological, cultural, economic, and in some cases, 'physical' or structural reasons, such as the limitations shown by Stevens' work on equal appearing intervals[58], or the arguments advanced by Simon noted above to account for the predominance of hierarchical structures.

4.1. Common preference orderings of judges

Garman and Kamien[59] suggest a procedure for varying the likelihood of one outcome being chosen over another. Rather than limiting P(n, m) to a function of *n* and *m*, only, they include an additional vector s, which they define as a 'culture.' To each vote V^t (outcome) a number s_t is assigned denoting the probability that a judge will select that vote. The resulting vector $\mathbf{s} = (s_1, s_2, \ldots s_{n!})$ is called a culture, where $\sum_{t=1}^{n!} s_t = 1$. An equivalent, and more suggestive approach might be to term this a price vector.

In Garman and Kamien's sense a culture is the measure of the similarity in individual preference orderings. Coombs'[60] unfolding technique is a more sophisticated attempt to solve this problem. Niemi[61] has applied this technique to the problem of ascertaining the probability of the paradox of voting if m_k of the *m* judges, share a common preference ordering which satisfies a common scale constructed according to Coombs' unfolding technique. While his calculations are restricted to the case of $n = 3$, the implications are clear. The probability of the paradox occurring is inversely proportional to the probability that judges share a common scale of values. His calculations for high *m*, with 2/3 of the preference orderings sharing a common J scale, are strongly concave. As *m* increases, if we hold the proportion of individuals with common preference orderings constant (at 2/3 or ~.70), the probability of the paradox decreases as the number, m, increases; and, decreases very rapidly for m greater than 95. Unfortunately:

'while the conditional probability of the paradox is near zero for moderate to large m, and 70-75 percent of the preference orderings satisfying a common J scale, the likelihood of getting less than this degree of unidimensionality by chance is sufficiently large so that the total probability of the paradox does not vanish but actually increases slightly as m increases.'[62]

The effect of a common scale of values is equivalent to either a reduction of n, the number of alternatives, or m, the number of judges, in the short run. However, in the long run (as n and m are allowed to increase) this only serves to moderate the rate at which the paradox becomes a problem. In the normal course of affairs, this may be sufficient to keep the probability of occurrence of the paradox sufficiently small that its occurrence is not a serious consideration.

Unfortunately, if there is no underlying similarity of preference, the original problem remains. This is clearly the case in many of the most critical areas of social conflict. It occurs both at the boundary areas between two different value systems, or societies, and in the dialectical development within a value system when, perhaps due to technological change, new preference orderings emerge faster than they can be reconciled to older structures of value. Both cultural lag and revolutionary conflict exhibit and illustrate such conflicts, occurring at different rates, but due to lack of a common value structure.

4.2. Single-peakedness assumptions

Another formulation of the problem emphasizes the criterion of single-peakedness[63] of preference orderings on a unidimensional scale. This is a more restrictive condition than simple unidimensionality which is required by attempts to use an interval scale rather than a simple ordinal scale. This formulation is a common restriction on majority decision problems. Unfortunately, group attitude functions are frequently not single-peaked. (They are generally not unidimensional either, but even over only one dimension, they are frequently not single-peaked, though they are customarily approximated by a single-peaked normal distribution.)

Modification of the original problem formulation with the introduction of an additional choice vector constrains the problem but does not alter its behavior over the long run. This is to be expected if we formulate the problem as an 0/1 integer programming, or optimization, problem rather than a Boolean satisfiability problem, since we then have only a larger, more complex, and possibly more ill conditioned, NP complete problem.

4.3. Connectivity and cyclical processes

If we can not 'solve' the cyclical majority problem, in the sense of resolving Arrow's Paradox, we are left with one alternative. We may accept it as the correct description of the decision processes, and resultant cyclical decision behavior, of large, complex, social systems characterized by (a) many decision makers who (b) order or choose from among many alternatives, but who (c) lack a common value structure or measure. The underlying reason behind the cyclical behavior of many social processes may be a group decision structure which produces cyclical majorities.

Cyclical majority decisions would at any point in time define a majority decision, but over a period of time would cycle through the entire set of alternatives. Levins[64] has noted a simulation of a network by Kauffman with properties equivalent to our formulation of the cyclical majority problem. The condition of complete connectivity is equivalent to our requirement that we allow judges preferences over *all* alternatives.

'A fundamental property, an essential feature of the system, is its connectivity. How many subsystems interact with a given subsystem and how strongly? Stuart Kauffman has investigated the behavior of a network of elements, each of which is either on or off, depending on the states of its inputs. Such a network will start from some arbitrary initial state (some elements on, some off) and change, until it settles down into some periodic behavior in which some elements are fixed permanently (on or off) while others form part of a cycle. Kaufman generated his network at random, specifying only the number of inputs per element, but not the particular connections. Then a boolean function was chosen at random to specify how the states of the inputs of each element determine its state. The most interesting result for our purposes is that with a high connectivity (many inputs per switch) the system goes into a very long cycle. For instance, if every element is connected to every other element in a network of n elements, the system could be in any one of 2^n states. In fact, it cycles through $2^{n/2}$ of these on the average.'[65]

Levins' conclusion parallels Arrow's Impossibility Theorem. 'The cyclic behavior of the network now is equivalent to logical contradiction in its circuitry. We suggest that spontaneous persistent activity in deterministic discrete systems is the equivalent of self-contradiction in the networks.'[66] Simon has also noted the dynamic properties of a 'nearly-decomposable'[67] hierarchical system.

'We see that the frequencies describing its dynamics can be *partially* ordered, and each subset of frequencies in the partial ordering (formally an equivalence class at some particular level of the ordering) can be associated with a specific subsystem in the partial ordering of system components. There will be, essentially, an isomorphism between the hierarchy of subsystems and the hierarchy of equivalence classes of frequencies describing the system, and particular frequencies will 'belong' to particular subsystems.'[68]

4.4. A time cost for decision processes

The notion of frequency associated with the dynamic behavior of highly interconnected Boolean networks suggests the introduction of a time cost for the decision process. A time cost for the decision process requires a point in time at which a single decision must be reached (as well as a maximum time for sets of decisions of the final or intermediate value aggregation). Such constraints do in fact exist in typical real world group decision problems, but were not imposed on our orginal formulation of the cyclical majority problem. We may modify our formulation of the problem by assuming: first, a time cost to aggregate the individual judges' decision matrices into the group decision matrix. We visualize each set of column summations as a $f(t)$ providing a partial ordering. Second, at some time (t_i) we will have exhausted the total time available to reach a decision, while not yet completely summing across all columns or all alternatives. The choice at this time is then based only on a partial ordering of the choices available at that time. Since we have at this time only a subset (n of m) of the complete set of choices, the partial set will be less likely to contain a complete cycle. If we impose an additional constraint that allows minor cycles (of length less than $(m-1)$) to be treated as indifference orders, we can almost always reach a decision as a $f(t_i)$ since, unless the decision period frequency is exactly m times the value aggregation frequency (for one alternative) we will always have a partial ordering. (The worst case would be a cycle of length n, giving total indifference over the partial order.) If we define our decision structures as a function of time, we may expect to reach a solution point. However, this is just what we would expect if we were modeling cyclical behavior.

Is this an 'irrelevant alternative?' In one sense, yes. However, to resolve a paradox we must in some way avoid self-reference and introduce some external context to the problem. The introduction of a temporal dimension is irrelevant to problems formulated such that the choices are not a function of time, or limited to alternatives defined so that time or the value of time is not included in the set of alternatives. However, for cybernetic and systems theory models, as well as the social processes they represent, time is rarely a truly irrelevant alternative. In fact, most cyclical behavior of social systems processes refer to temporal cycles.

The theoretical implications are perhaps even more significant. The cyclical majority problem provides a model of a control structure that is neither hierarchical nor 'completely' transitive. Yet, it is adequate to fulfill the requirements of decision and control needed by a cybernetic modeling involving both positive and negative feedback and causative communication. It indicates, rather, that cyclical behavior of a system may represent a structural rather than an environmental property of the system. Previous cybernetic models using formal automata to describe social systems as Turing machines have required a decision structure that implied a hierarchical structuring which mapped into the control function. The cyclical majority problem indicates the underlying decision structure which is the basis for the typically cyclical behavior exhibited by pluralistic cultures, markets and polities. A systemic, or holistic, organization does not imply the necessity of a complete dominance relation in the structural or architectural linkage between sub- and supra-system. A sub-system may also be a co-system.

4.5.1. An example: matrix management theory

We wish to note several specific processes which may be modeled explicitly as both hierarchical structures and cyclical majority decision processes. They reflect a specific interaction of social structure and group decision process. Recent work in management theory and organization design has introduced the matrix management model.[69] This model incorporates both traditional formal channels of authority and informal channels of communication and coordination among managers of equivalent (and perhaps inferior) rank but different functions. It reflects not only the well known role of informal channels of influence on decision making in hierarchical structures, but more recent project and task- or goal-oriented, rather than functional, approaches in management and organization thsseeory. Recently these models and empirical studies have begun to reveal the effects of embedding two different, and frequently contradictory, authority structures in the same institutional context. This not only produces expected conflicts between project lines of authority and functional lines of authority, it also gives rise to newer forms of collegial sharing of authority and new, formal and informal, group decision structures. Formally structured with two intersecting lines of authority, an explicit and intentional effort is made *not* to resolve the resulting conflicts. Rather project management authority structures are modeled as new 'row', or group coordination, decision structures intersecting the formal functional decision and authority structures represented by the 'columns' of the organizational matrix. We have at least two structural institutional 'judges' (as well as individual managers) negotiating over policy alternatives. The theory not only views the hierarchical structures as a decision matrix rather than a simple tree structure, the decision making processes, lacking a normative arbitrator or measure, follow the behavior exhibited by a cyclical majority model over time. Negotiation, conciliation, log-rolling and power sharing replace a command authority structure, where policy alternatives can only be rank-ordered rather than measured against an interval scale (e.g. the goal may be classical profit, but the profit alternatives may be long term or short term, project or division or corporate, national or international, etc.). Over time we observe a cyclical pattern of decision as the organization adjusts the frequency of specific choices relative to the period of the total decision process, which cycles through all alternatives in the decision space. There may also be second order decision processes superimposed over the first order processes, which will function to bring alternatives into and drop them from the decision space. But, the basic cyclical majority process provides a model of the decision processes driving the observed periodic behavior of ostensibly hierarchical structures.

4.5.2. Balance of power theory and requisite variety

At the other extreme of institutional complexity and structure, we find classical balance of power theory. Here the actors, or judges, are nation states, while the alternatives are generally alliances with or against other nation states. The theory itself dictates that a cyclical pattern of alliances is to result from a basic policy goal for actors which dictates resisting the dominance of any one actor in the system, and preserving rough equivalence of power among individual actors. Since relative power is the basic measure of alternative policies this is a prescription for an ordinal ranking of alternatives. With an ordinal ranking of alternatives, and more than two actors, (classical balance of power usually has at least three actors,) we have $n!$ alliance alternatives, and a cyclical majority decision problem.

If we include internal determinants of policy, such as factional alliances with external factions or nation states, as actors in such a model, we quickly arrive at an even larger number of judges and alternatives. The effect of international factional alliances on the stability of the international and domestic systems is well known, and accounts for the nation state's insistance on a monopoly of external political communication, as well as of force. If we allow factional subsystems of the hierarchically organized nation state subsystems to interact with the suprasystem directly, we will destabilize the nation state subsystems (and produce a matrix decision structure). We are also likely to destabilize, or change the frequency of the decision cycles exhibited by the international system. This is also to be expected if we use a cyclical majority decision model to explicate the balance of power process. Rosecrance uses a systems model to analyze the eighteenth and nineteenth century European balance of power.
(Roserance's model utilizes Ashby's law of requisite variety to formulate the constraints on the behavior of nation states.)[70] Emphasizing the importance of a hierarchical subsystem structure, he concludes, 'the present analysis calls attention to the internal organization of the state itself.... It prescribes domestic stability and internal peace as the vehicle of international stability and international peace.'[71] Rosecrance's results support the view of a cyclical majority decision process as an order preserving function over time, that allows for the preservation of a wider range of allowable choices in the decision set than the regulator, and the environment as the input generating demands on the system; clearly the law of requisite variety would specify a decision process that maximizes the variation in the set of decision alternatives over time. A cyclical majority decision process would do just this, providing over time a maximum of variety, and control, in the regulation of the environment. A more determinate structure would, as Ashby[72] has shown, function to eliminate alternatives over time, thus reducing the variety available to the regulators.

5. Conclusions: order preserving cyclical decision processes

Ashby's law of requisite variety, along with the recent solution to the graph coloring problem in the plane[73] (also an NP complete problem), suggests the conjecture that a noncyclical solution to a majority decision problem requires at least $(n + 1)$ judges for a decision over n alternatives. Such solutions might, however, still require considerable resources for large numbers of alternatives, as the recent computational solution to the four color problem demonstrated. This conjecture also tends to support our contention that cyclical dominance, of a very long period, as the number of choices and the number of judges increases, is in fact order preserving. These periods are equivalent to the cycles of Ashby's kinematic graph[74], which his law of requisite variety demonstrates are necessary to prevent reduction in the variety of a system.

5.1. The 'pretended autonomy' of criterion functions

These conclusions reflect two significant points which have been emphasized in Dooyeweerd's work.[75] If we exclude an 'imposed' solution based on 'irrelevant alternatives' external to the system, and an Arrow 'dictator' internal to the system, we expose the poverty of the pretended autonomy of a purely 'technical' solution to the problem. Such an approach requires the implicit or explicit elevation of one decision measure or subsystem value structure over the others. For a society to exhibit a continuing pattern of diversity, a transient but cyclical pattern of decision and control accommodating a pluralistic system of social spheres which substitutes temporary dominance for absolute hierarchy, and provides permanence of place for permanence of position or power, may be a sufficient, and perhaps even necessary model.

Dooyeweerd's work provides insights into and parallels our conclusions at several critical points. Perhaps most important is his emphasis on the absolute necessity for a basic value orientation which avoids the paradox which results from using numerous conflicting partial criterion functions. This paradox is the basis of the cyclical majority process and motivates our attention to it.

Rather than attempting to 'solve' the cyclical majority problem in a way which resolves Arrow's Paradox, we have attempted to show that it may exemplify a class of models of social systems which emphasize and accurately reflect actual system behavior; rather than impose an 'invisible dictator', perhaps in the form of some transitive hierarchical decision structure in the model, we accept a cyclical decision process as the result of the basic normative ambiguity which the logical decision structure reveals.

5.2. Cosystems and 'sphere sovereignty'

The concept of 'sphere sovereignty' contains not only an injunction against a totalitarian social structure, but the implication that ultimately social reality is not totalitarian, or reducible to a single hierarchy of decision structures by the use of a criterion function, no matter how complex. We thus suggest that a cyclical majority decision model may not only provide a more faithful short term model of various organizational decision processes, but may be a more accurate model of larger, more complex structures and their behavior over longer periods. More reductionistic[76] or totalitarian models, whose transitive value orderings may be mathematically appealing due to their tractability and computational economy, may also include 'hidden dictators' in their criterion functions or hierarchical structural features; while modeling a hierarchical structure accurately, we may fail to adequately describe its long term behavior if we insist on a solution that converges rather than oscillates. Such cyclical behavior may not be satisfactory for short term policy oriented problem solving, or social system design goals, but it may be a more accurate model of one aspect of social reality.

5.3. Summary

In summary, we return to our original question: 'Are societies Turing machines, or may we model them accurately with Turing machines?' An examination of the cyclical majority problem, and particularly its formulation as an NP complete problem, might lead us to the conclusion that for large, complex models over long periods, characterized by ordinal value criterion functions and more alternatives than judges in the decision space, our Turing machine may not halt, or if it does, not within a range of computation time of any interest to us.

In answering the question 'Are societies Turing machines?' the cyclical majority problem, an NP complete problem (as are cybernetic models of social systems) implies that such Turing machines may not halt, and almost certainly will not, within polynomial time. The cyclical majority problem is NP complete, and thus, equivalently reducible models of social systems are also NP complete problems. This implies that the value of recourse to technique in the solution of significant social problems by modeling may be restrained by its cost in time. It also indicates that we may successfully model social systems behavior with fidelity without requiring a 'completely' transitive solution to multi-attribute value aggregations. Such cyclical decision structures may even be uniquely appropriate to social systems models.

Notes

1. For a model exhibiting an explicit attempt to construct a finite automata see G. H. Kramer, 'An Impossibility Result Concerning the Theory of Decision Making' in J. Bernard (ed.) *Mathematical Applications in Political Science* Dallas, Texas: So. Meth. U. Press; 1966.
2. W. Buckley, *Sociology and Modern Systems Theory.* Englewood Cliffs, NJ: Prentice-Hall, 1967, and *Modern Systems Research for the Behavioral Scientist.* Chicago: Aldine, 1968.
3. T. Parsons, *The Social System.* Glencoe, Ill: The Free Press; 1951.
4. A. Etzioni, *The Active Society: A Theory of Societal and Political Processes.* New York: The Free Press, 1968. See also Breed, W., *The Self-Guiding Society.* New York: The Free Press, 1971.
5. K. W. Deutsch, *The Nerves of Government.* New York: The Free Press, 1963.
6. D. Easton, *A Systems Analysis of Political Life.* New York: Wiley, 1965.
7. J. W. Forrester, 'Understanding the Counter Intuitive Behavior of Social Systems' in J. Beishon and G. Peters (eds.), *Systems Behavior.* London: Harper and Row, 223-240, 1976,J. W. Forrester, *Urban Dynamics.* Cambridge, Mass.: The M.I.T. Press; 1971, J. W. Forrester, *World Dynamics.* Cambridge, Mass.: Wright-Allen Press, 1971.
8. D. H. Meadows, D. L. Meadows, J. Randers and W. W. Behrens III, *The Limits to Growth: A Report for the Club of Rome on the Predicament of Mankind.* New York: Signet, 1975.
9. M. Mesarovic and E. Pestel, *Mankind at the Turning Point: The Second Report to the Club of Rome.* New York: Signet, 1976.
10. W. R. Shaffer, *Computer Simulations of Voting Behavior,* New York: Oxford University Press, 1972.
11. I. de S. Pool, R. P. Abelson, and S. L. Popkin, *Candidates, Issues and Strategies: A Computer Simulation of the 1960 and 1964 Elections,* Cambridge, Mass.: The M.I.T. Press, 1965.
12. S. Z. Klauner, (ed.), *The Study of Total Societies*, New York: Doubleday, 1967.
13. R. P. Browning, 'Computer Programs as Theories of Political Processes.' *Journal of Politics* 24, 562-582, 1962.
14. E. Laszlo, *Introduction to Systems Philosophy: Toward a New Paradigm of Contemporary Thought*, New York: Harper and Row, 1972, and his *The Systems View of the World*, New York: Braziller, 1972.
15. E. Laszlo, *Introduction to Systems Philosophy*, 98-117 (see Note 14).
16. H. A. Simon, *The Shape of Automation for Men and Management*, Harper and Row, p. 102, 99-100, 1965.
17. H. H. Pattee, *Hierarchy Theory, the Challenge of Complex Systems*, New York: Braziller, p. xi, 1973.

18. H. A. Simon, *The Shape of Automation*, p. 70-71 (see Note 16).
19. *Ibid*, p. 72.
20. See E. Yourdon and L. L. Constantine, *Structured Design*, New York: Yourdon, 1976; also O. J. Dahl, E. W. Dijkstra, and C. A. R. Hoare, *Structured Programming*, New York: Academic Press; 1972, especially Part III, 'Hierarchical Program Structures' by O. J. Dahl and C. A. R. Hoare.
21. H. A. Simon, *The Shape of Automation*, p. 101 (see Note 16).
22. See A. C. Shaw, *The Logical Design of Operating Systems*, Englewood Cliffs, NJ: Prentice-Hall, 1974, especially Chap. 8, 'The Deadlock Problem'.
23. See E. W. Dijkstra, *A Discipline of Programming*, Englewood Cliffs, NJ: Prentice-Hall, 1976, and 'Guarded Commands, Nondeterminacy and Formal Derivation of Programs' in R. T. Yeh (ed.), *Current Trends in Programming Methodology*, Vol. I: *Software Specification and Design*, Englewood Cliffs, NJ: Prentice-Hall, 1977.
24. See E. Yourdon and L. L. Constantine, *Structured Design*, esp. Chap. 18, 'Homologous and Incremental Structures' (Note 20) and O. J. Dahl, E. W. Dijkstra, and C. A. R. Hoare, *Structured Programming*, 'Hierarchical Program Structures' by O. J. Dahl and C. A. R. Hoare (Note 20).
    Simon also refers to similar program structures as 'productions' in H. H. Pattee (ed.) *Hierarchy Theory*, 'The Organization of Complex Systems', p. 19 (see Note 17).
25. See J. Martin, *Computer Data-Base Organization*, Englewood Cliffs, NJ: Prentice Hall, 1975, especially Chap. 20, 'Chains and Ring Structures'.
26. K. Arrow, *Social Choice and Individual Values*, New Haven: Yale University Press, 2nd edition, 1963.
27. W. H. Riker, 'Voting and the Summation of Preferences: An Interpretive Bibliographical Review of Selected Developments during the Last Decade.' *American Political Science Review* 55 (December): 900-911, 1961.
28. G. Th. Guilbaud, 'Theories of the General Interest, and the Logical Problem of Aggregations' in P. F. Lazarsfeld and N. W. Henry (eds.) *Readings in Mathematical Social Science.* Cambridge, Mass.: The M.I.T. Press, 262-308, 1966.
29. R. G. Niemi, and H. F. Weisberg, 'A Mathematical Solution for the Probability of the Paradox of Voting.' *Behavioral Science* 13, Nr. 4, (July): 317-323, 1968.
30. M. B. Garman and M. I. Kamien, 'The Paradox of Voting: Probability Calculations.' *Behavioral Science* 13, Nr. 4 (July): 306-316, 1968.
31. F. S. Roberts, *Discrete Mathematical Models*, Englewood Cliffs, NJ: Prentice-Hall, 1976, especially Chap. 7, 'Group Decision Making'.
32. C. D. Campbell and G. Tullock, 'The Paradox of Voting – A Possible Method of Calculation.' *American Political Science Review* 60, 684-685, 1966.
33. D. Klahr, 'A Computer Simulation of the Paradox of Voting.' *American Political Science Review* 60, Nr. 2 (June): 384-390, 1966.
34. J. E. Pomeranz and R. L. Weill, Jr., 'The Cyclical Majority Problem.' *Communications of the ACM* 13, Nr. 4 (April): 251-255, 1970.
35. A. Kirman and D. Sondermann, 'Arrow's Theorem, Many Agents and Invisible Dictators.' *Journal of Economic Theory* 5, 267-277, 1972.
36. B. Hansson, 'The existence of Group Preference Functions,' *Public Choice* XXVIII, (Winter): 89-98, 1976.
37. P. C. Fishburn, 'Arrow's Impossibility Theorem: Concise Proof and Infinite Voters.' *Journal of Economic Theory* 2, 103-106, 1970.
38. B. Hansson, 'The existence of Group Preference Functions.' *Public Choice*, pp. 89-98 (see Note 36).
39. J. E. Pomeranz and R. L. Weill Jr., 'The Cyclical Majority Problem.' *Communications of the ACM.* pp. 251-255 (see Note 34).

40. R. M. Karp, 'Reducibility Among Combinatorial Problems' in R. E. Miller and J. W. Thatcher, (eds.), *Complexity of Computer Computations*, New York: Plenum Press, 85-103, 1972.
41. R. G. Niemi and H. F. Weisberg, 'A Mathematical Solution for the Probability of the Paradox of Voting.' *Behavioral Science* 13, Nr. 4, (July): 320, 1968.
R. G. Niemi and H. F. Weisberg, *Probability Models of Collective Decision*, Columbus, Ohio: Merrill, 1972, especially Part 3, 'The Paradox of Voting,' pp. 181-272.
42. M. B. Garman and M. I. Kamien, 'The Paradox of Voting: Probability Calculations.' *Behavioral Science* 13, Nr. 4 (July): 313, 1968.
43. P. C. Fishburn, *The Theory of Social Choice*, Princeton, NJ: Princeton University Press, 1977, and his 'Arrow's Impossibility Theorem: Concise Proof and Infinite Voters.' *Journal of Economic Theory* 2, 103-106, 1970.
44. B. Hansson, 'The Existence of Group Preference Functions.' *Public Choice*, p. 97 (see Note 36).
45. See P. K. Pattanaik, *Voting and Collective Choice*, Cambridge, England: Cambridge University Press, 1971.
46. K. Arrow, *Social Choice and Individual Values* (see Note 26). Compare especially Theorem 2, p. 59, and Theorem 3 and its corollary, p. 63.
47. For a formal treatment of Turing machines, see M. Minsky, *Computation: Finite and Infinite Machines*, Englewood Cliffs, NJ: Prentice-Hall, 1967. For a discussion of NP completeness and complexity hierarchies, see A. V. Aho,, J. E. Hopcraft and J. D. Ullman, *The Design and Analysis of Computer Algorithms*, Reading, Mass.: Addison-Wesley, 1974, also M. A. Arbib, *Theories of Abstract Automata*, Englewood Cliffs, NJ: Prentice-Hall, 1969.
48. B. Weide, 'A Survey of Analysis Techniques for Discrete Algorithms,' ACM *Computing Surveys* 9, Nr. 4, (December): 291-314, 1977.
49. *Ibid*, p. 306.
50. *Ibid*, p. 307.
51. *Ibid*. Weide also notes: 'A language L_1 is "polynomially reducible" to L_2 if there is a deterministic polynomial-time algorithm which transforms a string x into a string $f(x)$ such that x is in L_1 iff $f(x)$ is in L_2.'
52. R. M. Karp, 'Reducibility Among Combinatorial Problems,' *Complexity of Computer Computations* (see Note 40), pp. 85-103.
53. B. Weide, 'A Survey of Analysis Techniques for Discrete Algorithms,' ACM *Computing Surveys* (see Note 48), p. 307.
54. T. C. T. Kotiah and D. I. Steinberg, 'Occurrences of Cycling and Other Phenomena Arising in a Class of Linear Programming Models.' *Communications of the* ACM 20, Nr. 2 (February): 107-112,1977.
55. R. L. Keeney and H. Raiffa, *Decisions with Multiple Objectives: Preferences and Value Tradeoffs*, New York: Wiley, 1976, especially Chap. 10, 'Aggregation of Individual Preferences,' and Section 10.6.1, 'The Supra Decision Maker Model.'
56. See P. K. Pattanaik, *Voting and Collective Choice* (Note 45). Also Y. Murakami, *Logic and Social Choice*, New York: Dover, 1968.
57. G. Tullock, 'The General Irrelevance of the General Impossibility Theorem.' *Quarterly Journal of Economics* 81, 256-270, 1967.
58. S. S. Stevens, 'Measurement, Psychophysics and Utility,' in C. W. Churchman and P. Ratoush (eds.) *Measurement: Definitions and Theories*, New York: Wiley, 18-63, 1959.
59. M. B. Garman and M. I. Kamien, 'The Paradox of Voting: Probability Calculations,' *Behavioral Science*, 306-316 (Note 42).
60. C. H. Coombs, *A Theory of Data*, New York: Wiley, 1964.
61. R. G. Niemi, 'Majority Decision Making with Partial Unidimensionality,' *American Political Science Review* 63, Nr. 2 (June): 488-497, 1969.

62. *Ibid*, pp. 493-494.
63. *Ibid*, p. 488. Niemi defines single-peakedness as follows:
'A set of preference orderings is single-peaked if there is an ordering of the alternatives on the abscissa such that when utility or degree of preference is indicated by the ordinate, each preference ordering can be represented by a curve which changes its direction at most once, from up to down (i.e. has at most one peak).'
64. R. Levins, 'The Limits of Complexity' in *Hierarchy Theory*, p. 114, (see Note 17), also S. A. Kauffman, 'Metabolic Stability and Epigenesis in Randomly Constructed Genetic Nets.' *Journal of Theoretical Biology* 22, 437-467.
65. *Ibid*, pp. 114-115.
66. *Ibid*, p. 115.
67. See A. Ando, F. M. Fisher and H. A. Simon, *Essays on the Structure of Social Science Models*, Cambridge, Mass.: The M.I.T. Press, 1963, for an extensive discussion of 'near-decomposability'.
68. H. A. Simon, 'The Organization of Complex Systems,' *Hierarchy Theory*, pp. 15-16 (see Note 17).
69. See L. R. Sayles, 'Matrix Management, the Structure with a Future,' *Organizational Dynamics* 5, Nr. 2 (August): 2-10, 1976; P. R. Lawrence, H. F. Kolodny and S. M. Davis, 'The Human Side of the Matrix.' *Organizational Dynamics* 6, Nr. 1 (Summer): 43-61, 1977; J. R. Galbraith, 'Matrix Organization Design.' *Business Horizons* (February): 21-40, 1971; C. Argyris, 'Today's Problems with Tomorrows Organizations,' *The Journal of Management Studies* (March): 84-101, 1973; and S. M. Davis and P. R. Lawrence, *Matrix*, New York: Macmillan, 1977.
70. R. N. Rosecrance, *Action and Reaction in World Politics*, Boston: Little, Brown, p. 222, 1963.
71. *Ibid*, p. 306.
72. W. R. Ashby, *An Introduction to Cybernetics*, New York: Wiley, 1963, especially Chap. 13.
73. See K. Appel, and W. Haken, 'The Solution of the Four-Color Map Problem.' *Scientific American* 237, Nr. 4 (October): 108-121, 1977.
74. W. R. Ashby, *An Introduction to Cybernetics* (see Note 72), 22-23, also Chaps. 5 and 7.
75. See H. Dooyeweerd, *In the Twilight of Western Thought: Studies in the Pretended Autonomy of Philosophical Thought.* Grand Rapids, Mich.: Baker, 1960, and his *Transcendental Problems in Philosophic Thought*. Grand Rapids, Mich.: Baker, 1953.
76. Simon also cautions against a 'Laplacian' reductionism. See H. A. Simon, 'The Organization of Complex Systems' in *Hierarchy Theory*, pp. 24-27 (see Note 17).

Dialectics and catastrophe

Martin Zwick

1. Introduction

The Catastrophe Theory of René Thom and E. C. Zeeman[1] suggests a mathematical interpretation of certain aspects of Hegelian and Marxist dialectics. Specifically, the three 'classical' dialectical principles[2], (1) the transformation of quantity into quality, (2) the unity and struggle of opposites, and (3) the negation of negation, can be modeled with the seven '*elementary catastrophes*'[3] given by Thom, especially the catastrophes known as the 'cusp' and the 'butterfly.' Far from being empty metaphysics or scholasticism, as critics have argued, the dialectical principles embody genuine insights into a class of phenomena, insights which can now be expressed within a precise mathematical formalism. This fact does not, however, support the claim that these principles, possibly modified or supplemented, constitute *the* laws of motion for human thought and for natural and social processes – or even just the last of these.

There is, of course, an enormous and diverse literature on dialectics. The three Hegelian 'laws' will be focused upon, somewhat arbitrarily, because they offer a clear context for discussion. These laws are centainly only one particular reification of a more general framework for analysis and synthesis, which has been extensively developed by writers and philosophers associated with the Communist movement[4], the independent left, and the academic research community. This paper will give only a preliminary demonstration of the close relationship which exists between dialectics and catastrophe theory. A more systematic examination of the dialectical literature from a catastrophe theoretic perspective will be undertaken at a later date.

Some remarks are in order on the nature of catastrophe theory. This theory can be used in a variety of ways ranging from (a) rigorous applications, where the underlying assumptions of the theory can be validated, and where quantitative explanation and prediction is sought, to (b) cases where catastrophe models are invoked *a priori,* but are empirically and quantitatively assessed, to (c) more qualitative modeling of phenomena using the catastrophe archetypes (with perhaps an aspiration to future quantitative treatment), to (d) purely symbolic or metaphoric use of the visual imagery of the theory. Most of the discussion in this paper will be at the qualitative end of this spectrum, but more mathematical aspects of Thom's theory are also relevant. For example, phase transitions, such as the boiling or freezing of liquids, are frequently cited in the Marxist literature as examples of dialectical phenomena, and these phenomena can be described by catastrophe theory (Dodson, 1976; Schulman and Revzen, 1972) at quite a rigorous and quantitative level of analysis.

In the next section, a brief account of catastrophe theory is given by introducing the cusp, the most widely used of the catastrophe types. An interpretation of the three classical dialectical laws is developed in terms of the cusp (Section 3), and applied to the writings of Marx and Engels on political economy and history (Section 4). Here it is necessary to acknowledge in advance – indeed to stress – that the catastrophe-theoretic interpretation does not add new content to the Marxian analyses, but merely highlights their underlying coherence, via a rich system of visual metaphor. That is, like dialectics, catastrophe theory provides a language for modeling and a method of exposition. In Section 5, the butterfly catastrophe is introduced and used to describe a dialectic different from that of the cusp, one in which the struggle of opposites can lead to the creation or dissolution of an independent synthesis. Finally, Section 6 gives a summary and indicates directions for future work.

2. The cusp catastrophe

Thom's theory is about transitions from continuous cause-effect relationships to discontinuous ones. Specifically, the theory describes seven ways ('elementary catastrophes') in which either one or two *'behavior'* variables (effects) can change discontinuously as a result of continuous variation of up to four *'control'* parameters (causes)[5]. The seven catastrophe types, in order of increasing complexity, are: fold, cusp, swallowtail, butterfly, hyperbolic umbilic, elliptic umbilic, and parabolic umbilic. This paper will consider the cusp and butterfly (figures 1 and 4), which offer fundamentally different interpretations of dialectics. The other elementary catastrophes may also model dialectical phenomena, but will not be discussed.

In the cusp catastrophe, there is one behavior variable and two control parameters whose relationship can be modeled with the 'catastrophe machine' (Zeeman, 1976, 1977) shown in figure 1a.

In this model, two rubber bands are attached to a disk which can rotate about its center. The other end of the first rubber band is fixed while the second has a free end (the '*control point*') which can move about in the plane of the figure. The rotation angle of the disk (x) is the behavior variable, and the control parameters are the coordinates (a,b) of the control point. If this point is moved across the cusp-shaped '*bifurcation set*' from point 1 to point 7, the disk angle will change gradually until point 6, where it will undergo a discontinuous rotational jump ('*catastrophe*').

Figure 1b gives one interpretation of what is happening: The system is assumed always to be at equilibrium in a local minimum (initially, α) of some energy function. As the control point moves, the topography of the energy function changes. At point 2, i.e. when the control point first enters the bifurcation set[6], an inflection point appears, which, at 3, deepens into a second minimum, β. This minimum corresponds to a different equilibrium value for the angular variable, x. At point 4, the depth of the two minima are equal, but at 5, the second state is actually preferred, i.e. if one agitated the disk sufficiently, it would jump from α to β . But if the control point moves gradually, the system does not switch to the new state until its own local minimum disappears (point 6). If one reversed the direction of motion, the disk would rotate slowly, but remain in the range of values we call minimum β, until point 2, where it would undergo a discontinuous flip to minimum α. Thus, on one side of the bifurcation set (point 1) there is only the α minimum, and on the other side (point 7) only the β minimum. Inside the bifurcation set, the system can occupy either minimum, depending upon the previous motion of the control point.

Figure 1c represents additional aspects of this process. The bifurcation set here is the same as the one shown in Figure 1a, but the diagram introduces an alternative coordinate system which may be used to specify the position of the control point. (For the coordinate system shown earlier in Figure 1a, the parameters a' and b' are called '*splitting*' and '*normal*' factors, respectively. In the present arrangement, a' and b' are called '*conflicting*' factors.) As the control point moves on a '*control surface*' across the bifurcation set, a '*behavior point*' moves along with it, constrained to lie on the '*behavior surface*' directly above the control point[7].

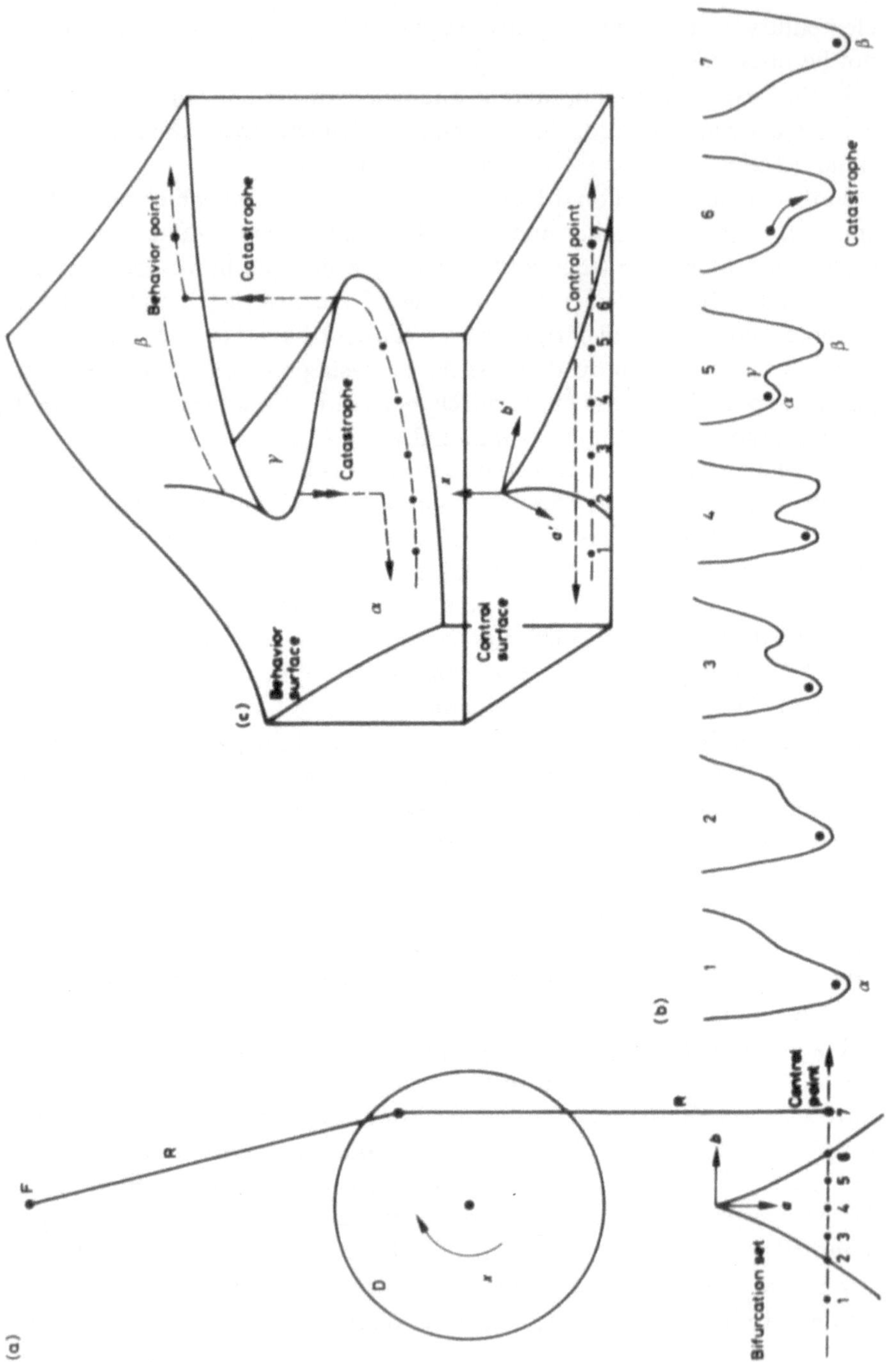
(a)
F
R
D
x
R
Bifurcation set
a
b
1 2 3 4 5 6 7
Control point
(b)
1
2
3
4
5
6
7
α
γ
β
Catastrophe
(c)
Behavior surface
Control surface
α
γ
β
Catastrophe
Behavior point
Catastrophe
x
a'
b'
Control point
1 2 3 4 5 6 7

The vertical height of the behavior point gives the value of the behavior variable, x, and the catastrophe which occurs at point 6 corresponds to this point jumping from the lower sheet onto the upper. (For motion in the reverse direction, from 7 to 1, it jumps downward, as shown.) Note that the intermediate region (γ) in the S-shaped fold is inaccessible; this corresponds to the local maxima shown in figure 1b. Also, a path which does not actually cross the bifurcation set, or which enters and leaves this region at the same boundary, will not result in any discontinuity.

The occurrence of the jump at different points for forward and reverse paths is an illustration of the property of 'hysteresis'. The existence inside the bifurcation set of two possible equilibrium states (or, more generally,

Figure 1. A model of the cusp catastrophe (Zeeman, 1976, 1977). (a) A 'catastrophe machine.' F is a fixed point; D, a disk; R, a rubber band; x, the behavior variable; a and b are splitting and normal factor coordinate axes which specify the location of the control point. As the control point crosses the bifurcation set, the rotation angle of the disk changes discontinuously (a 'catastrophe.') (b) Changes in the energy function for the motion of the control point shown in (a). α and β are energy minima, γ an energy maximum; inflection points occur at 2 and 6. (c) The control and behavior surfaces. As the control point moves accros the bifurcation set (same as in (a)) on the control surface, the behavior point follows above it on the behavior surface. The upper and lower sheets of the behavior surface correspond to the α and β minima; the central sheet is inaccessible to the behavior point and corresponds to γ. The height of the behavior point specifies the rotation angle, x. See Section 2 for additional discussion. In all figures, dashed arrows are control point trajectories (double arrows indicate rapid motion); solid årrows specify coordinate axes.

Figure 1. A model of the cusp catastrophe (Zeeman, 1976, 1977).*

Figure 1a. A 'catastrophe machine.' F is a fixed point; D, a disk; R, a rubber band; x, the behavior variable; a and b are splitting and normal factor coordinate axes which specify the location of the control point. As the control point crosses the bifurcation set, the rotation angle of the disk changes discontinuously (a 'catastrophe').

Figure 1b. Changes in the energy function for the motion of the control point shown in 1a. α and β are energy minima, γ an energy maximum; inflection points occur at 2 and 6.

Figure 1c. The control and behavior surfaces. As the control point moves across the bifurcation set (same as in 1a) on the control surface, the behavior point follows above it on the behavior surface. The upper and lower sheets of the behavior surface correspond to the α and β minima; the central sheet is inaccessible to the behavior point and corresponds to γ. The height of the behavior point specifies the rotation angle, x. See Section 2 for additional discussion.

* For Figures 1-4, dashed arrows are control point trajectories. Double arrows indicate rapid motion. Solid arrows specify coordinate axes.

the split of the behavior surface into upper and lower sheets) is referred to as '*bimodality*'. The fact that the system does not change its state immediately after point 4, even though minimum β is favored, and does so only when it crosses the other boundary of the bifurcation set, is called '*delay*'. The vertex of the cusp in the control surface, and the corresponding point at which the behavior surface bifurcates, are known as 'singularities'. Very small changes in the motion of the behavior point near the singularity can lead to passage onto either the lower or upper surface; this is known as '*divergence*'.

It should be stressed that the path of the control point is in no way dictated by the theory, but must be provided anew for each phenomenon being modeled. Also a coordinate system for the control point must be chosen. The reader might glance ahead to Figures 3a and 3b to see some other possible control point trajectories. The first of these uses conflicting control factors, each favoring one particular equilibrium state. (The bifurcation set is then an arena of conflict.) The second uses normal and splitting factors. The first parameter effectively determines which state the system is in, while the second specifies the separation between these states i.e. the gap between the upper and lower behavior surfaces.

Actually, the properties of 'delay', and the discontinuity of the transition between the two possible minima, are not strictly required in the cusp catastrophe, even when the bifurcation set is completely traversed. Some systems may undergo a transition at or close to the moment when a deeper minimum appears (e.g. immedately beyond point 4 in Figure 1). In such cases the transition occurs inside the bifurcation set, and this is known as the 'Maxwell' convention. Also if the system consists of many units, each of which can undergo an independent transition between the two states, then the population of units, taken collectively, can exhibit a smooth transition curve. This would resemble a hypothetical path parallel to the one shown in Figure 1, but 'behind' the singularity, i.e. before the behavior surface has bifurcated into two sheets.

These are the essentials of the cusp catastrophe. It might be instructive to cite a few of the applications which have been made of this model. The phenomenon of phase transitions has already been mentioned as a standard example of dialectics, given by Hegel, Engels, and most, if not all, subsequent Marxist writers on this subject. Here temperature and pressure are conflicting factors. The phenomenon exhibits delay in transitions from supersaturated states, but more typically follows the Maxwellian mode. Other uses or illustrations of the cusp, with varying degrees of mathematical and empirical elaboration, have included the analysis of the nerve impulse, the heartbeat, stock market cycles, embryological differentiation, euler buckling, military conflict and peacemaking, neurological and physiological rhythms, light caustics, and so on (Zeeman, 1976, 1977).

3. The dialectical laws

3.1. Quantity and quality

The relationship of the cusp catastrophe to the classical laws of dialects is summarized in Figure 2.

The first law, 'the transformation of quantity to quality,' is close to, though not exactly synonymous with, the generation of discontinuous effects from continuous causes. The two behavioral modes of the cusp are usually qualitatively distinct, as in the phase transition example, where the two regions of density correspond to the gas and liquid states. From a dialectical perspective, change of the quantitative nature, involving 'mere' increase of decrease, which does not alter the basis character of the system cannot go on indefinitely, but at a certain point (Hegel's 'nodal line'), alsways leads to a qualitative transformation (or 'leap'). Water, when heated, does not go on getting hotter and hotter indefinitely, but at a certain critical temperature, begins to turn into steam, and undergoes a qualitative change from liquid to gas. The dialectical description is identical to the catastrophe theoretic one. Hegel's 'nodal line' is the bifurcation set, and his 'leap' is the catastrophe.

The transformation of quantity into quality can also be seen in the cusp property of divergence, wherein small quantitative differences in the path of the control point are amplified and yield qualitatively different results. Evolutionary speciation, a phenomenon which exhibits this property, has recently been the subject of catastrophe theoretic study (Dodson, 1976; Waddington, 1974). And, as Graham notes (1971):

'To Marx and Engels, Darwin's theory of evolution was an important illustration of the principle of the transition from quantity to quality. This tenet as a part of the Hegelian dialectic preceded Darwin, of course, but Marx and Engels considered Darwinism a vindication of the dialectical process. In the course of natural selection, different species developed from common ancestors; this transition could be considered an example of accumulated quantitative changes resulting in a qualitative change, the latter change being marked by the moment when the diverging groups could not longer interbreed.'

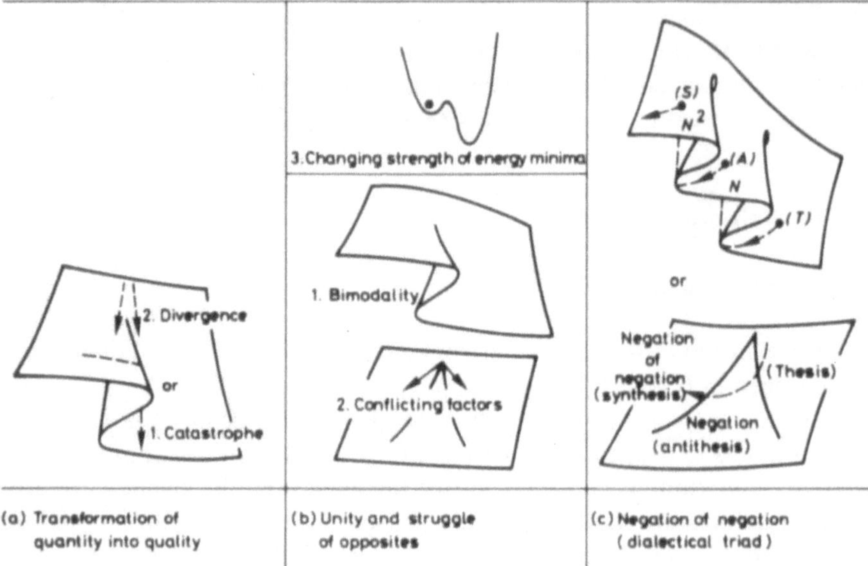

Figure 2. The three dialectical laws interpreted in terms of the cusp. (a) The transformation of quantity into quality is illustrated in the property of catastrophe *or* that of divergence, though some phenomena may exhibit both of these. (b) The unity and struggle of opposites is manifest in the three linked properties which are shown, except that control factors may sometimes be given in terms of normal and splitting factors. (c) The negation of negation may be given the first *or* the second interpretation above. (The lower diagram is not the control surface for the upper.) See Section 3 for additional discussion.

Figure 2. The three dialectical laws interpreted in terms of the cusp.

Figure 2a. The transformation of quantity into quality is illustrated in the property of catastrophe *or* that of divergence, though some phenomena may exhibit both of these.

Figure 2b. The unity and struggle of opposites is manifest in the three linked properties which are shown, except that control factors may sometimes be given in terms of normal and splitting factors.

Figure 2c. The negation of negation may be given the first *or* the second interpretation above. (The lower diagram is not the control surface for the upper.) See Section 3 for additional discussion.

3.2. Interpenetration of opposites

In dialectics, the concept of 'development' is distinguished from that of growth to indicate that real change is not a smooth process, but one in which phases of gradual evolution are interrupted by breaks in continuity. This development is said to take place through the unity and struggle – or to use Engel's original formulation, through the mutual interpenetration – of opposites. Linked opposites appear in the cusp model in several ways (Figure 2b): (1) The behavior surface is bimodal beyond the point of singularity, and the two behavioral possibilities overlap inside the region of the bifurcation set. Also, the inaccessibility of the central surface (γ in Figure 1c) indicates the impossibility of compromise (intermediate values of the behavior variable) between the two modes. (2) The control parameters, when given as conflicting factors (e.g. temperature and pressure in the phase transition case) oppose one another but act jointly on the system. If one factor is dominant or exclusively present, it will lead the system into one or the other of the alternate states. Since the regions of dominance overlap, if both factors are approximately in balance, there is a struggle of opposites. (3) Inside the bifurcation set, the potential function has two minima, which arise from the interpenetration of the domains of influence of the conflicting factors. One minimum corresponds to the actual state of the system, the other to a potential alternative state[8]. In the changing relative strength of the two minima, there is the struggle between the old which is dying away or disappearing and the new which is being born or developing. In the reversal of the relations of dominance between the opposites, one quality comes to replace another[9].

This developmental process is actually the 'internal content' of the transformation of quantity into quality, i.e. after a long series of gradual changes, the victory of the new over the old occurs suddenly and discontinuously. (Actually, both dialectics and catastrophe theory allow also for qualitative change which is continuous but at least more rapid than the events which lead up to it.) After the qualitative change or catastrophic 'leap', the process continues to unfold and to complete itself, according to the detailed circumstances of the situation.

3.3. Negation of negation

The third dialectical law can be given at least two different interpretations in terms of the cusp (Figure 2c).

(1) The process continues beyond the first transformation, i.e. each negation represents a qualitative leap. This can be represented by concatenating two or more cusps. (If they are connected in a spiral pattern,

this will also suggest the idea that the second negation restores some earlier condition, but at a higher level.) (2) The negation of negation can also be seen within a single cusp in the following sequence. Initially, there is a single potential minimum, and corresponding behavioral mode, and the uncontested dominance of one of the conflicting factors. Upon entry into the bifurcation set, this condition is negated, and replaced with contradiction, bimodality, and strife. Finally, the struggle of opposites culminates in a qualitative jump: the system experiences the second negation, unimodality is restored – but in the new state.

Here also is an interpretation of the familiar triad of thesis, antithesis, and synthesis, which is closely related to the principle of negation of negation. The triad is not a prominent feature of the dialectics of Engels and Marx, who mocked its 'wooden' uses, but it is found, at least implicitly, in their writings. It can be given two possible interpretations. In the first, thesis, antithesis, and synthesis are the three surfaces of two concatenated cusps. In the second, the region ouside the bifurcation set (prior to entry into it) is the thesis, the region inside it is the antithesis, i.e. the domain of contradiction, and the region on the other side of it (into which the control point emerges, causing the 'leap') is the synthesis.

4. The Cusp of contradiction

4.1. Dialectics of capitalism

The cusp interpretation of the dialectical principles can be illustrated with some examples selected from (or related to) the writings of Marx and Engels on political economy (Engels, 1941, 1968; Marx, 1904, 1947, 1967, 1968).

Generally any system which undergoes a discontinuous change between one stable state and another can be modeled with the cusp, so we can apply it to the transition between systems of production, and specifically to the transition from capitalism to socialism which Marx predicted and worked towards. There are two ways in which this transition is described. One might be called the 'deep structure' of the process, and is cast in terms of an underlying dialectic between forces and relations of production. The second provides the 'surface structure,' i.e. what is plainly visible. Here the focus is on the actual process by which the relations of production are altered, and on the agents of historical change, the social classes.

The struggle between the principal opposing classes can obviously be represented on the cusp, as shown in Figure 3a, where the strength of the bourgeoisie and the proletariat are the conflicting control factors. The path of the control point in this figure approximately characterizes the dialectical conception of how systems develop and become transformed. First, one control variable increases and establishes its dominance. This process then gives rise inevitably to a growth in strength of an opposing factor, and simultaneously to a gradual slowing in the increase of the first. That is, the success of the system leads invariably, first to the emergence and then to the intensification of inner contradictions. Finally, the second factor, via a catastrophic jump, achieves dominance, and the system is transformed.

The analysis given by Turner (1974) of 'the dialectical causal imagery' gives one possible account of the sequence of events through which this process passes. The stages are approximately as follows: (1) An initial form of social organization; in the present case, the emergence of the capitalist property relations; (2) Domination of the propertied social classes over other classes; (3) Objective opposition of interests between classes over distribution of property and power; (4) Consciousness of this opposition of interests by the dominated class; (5) Politicization of the subjugated population and increased tension; (6) Revolutionary conflict; (7) Social reorganization and the redistribution of property and power.

This sequence of stages is modeled by the path of the control point through points 1 to 7 in Figure 3a. It is at point 4, where the opposition of interests is consciously perceived, that the bifurcation set is entered. For the first time, there exist two possible equilibria, a capitalist and a socialist one, although the former is still strongly favored. The struggle of opposites intensifies, but even after the balance of power has shifted, the old equilibrium state persists, until 'its minimum' completely and suddenly disappears. The overall process exemplifies many features of the catastrophe theoretic interpretation of the dialectical laws, given in the previous section. Needless to say, this analysis is a general one; it can be applied to any dyadic conflict situation and to conflict theories which differ from the Marxian model.

The divergence property of the cusp may also be used to model the process of polarization (Figure 3b), and the shifting boundary between classes (Figure 3c). This latter figure makes use of a slightly more complex form of cusp geometry, used by Zeeman (1977) for analysis of embryological and ecological phenomena. Marx's account of the proletarianization of the petty-bourgeoisie and of the inevitable decrease in the number of capitalists is simply pictured. The figure almost suggests the surprise of

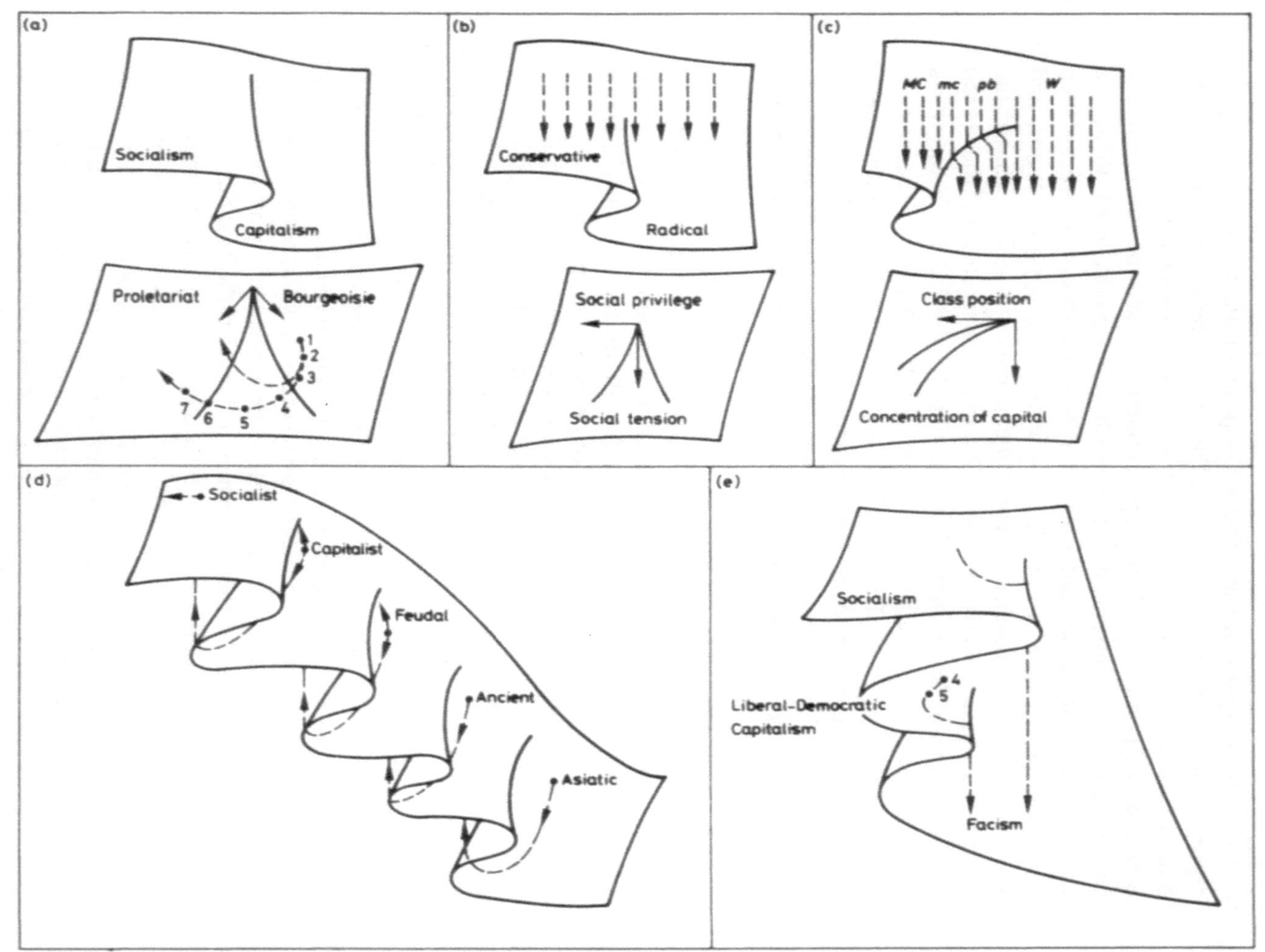
(a)
Socialism
Capitalism
Proletariat
Bourgeoisie
1
2
3
4
5
6
7
(b)
Conservative
Radical
Social privilege
Social tension
(c)
MC
mc
pb
W
Class position
Concentration of capital
(d)
Socialist
Capitalist
Feudal
Ancient
Asiatic
(e)
Socialism
Liberal-Democratic
Capitalism
4
5
Facism

Figure 3. Some Marxian applications of the cusp. (a) Class struggle leading to socialism represented as a trajectory on the control surface. Conflicting factors are the strengths of the bourgeois and working classes. The behavior variable is some of the socialization of production. The control point path with the smaller arc shows an unlikely yet conceivable alternative trajectory. (b) Polarization. Political orientation, the behavior variable, becomes increasingly polarized along lines of power and privilege as social tension grows (e.g. point 5 in the trajectory shown in (a)). (c) Proletarianization of the petty bourgeois (pb) and minor capitalists (mc) with the concentration of capital and expansion of monopoly. MC represents major capitalists; W, workers. Similar to the polarization shown in (b), but altered cusp geometry gives a shifting boundary between the dominant and subordinate classes. (d) A modified and highly idealized Marxian view of historical stages, showing mainly discontinuous changes between systems of production, but the possibility also of alternative routes. (e) The secondary cusp of fascism. Entry into the bifurcation set of the capitalism-socialism transition, e.g. point 4 and 5 in the trajectory of (a) can trigger a strong reaction. This can generate a new topological singularity, with a 'secondary' cusp which splits the capitalism surface into liberal democratic and fascist alternatives. Reversal of the control point motion, either before or after socialism is reached, may cause sudden transition not to democratic capitalism but to fascism. See discussion in Section 4.

Figure 3. Some Marxian applications of the cusp.

Figure 3a. Class struggle leading to socialism represented as a trajectory on the control surface. Conflicting factors are the strengths of the bourgeois and working classes. The behavior variable is some of the socialization of production. The control point path with the smaller arc shows an unlikely yet conceivable alternative trajectory.

Figure 3b. Polarization. Political orientation, the behavior variable, becomes increasingly polarized along lines of power and privilege as social tension grows (e.g. point 5 in the trajectory shown in 3a.)

Figure 3c. Proletarianization of the petty bourgeois (pb) and minor capitalists (mc) with the concentration of capital and expansion of monopoly. MC represents major capitalists; W, workers. Similar to the polarization shown in 3b, but altered cusp geometry gives a shifting boundary between the dominant and subordinate classes.

Figure 3d. A modified and highly idealized Marxian view of historical stages, showing mainly discontinuous changes between systems of production, but the possibility also of alternative routes.

Figure 3e. The secondary cusp of fascism. Entry into the bifurcation set of the capitalism-socialism transition, e.g. point 4 and 5 in the trajectory of 3a, can trigger a strong reaction. This can generate a new topological singularity, with a 'secondary' cusp which splits the capitalism surface into liberal democratic and fascist alternatives. Reversal of the control point motion, either before or after socialism is reached, may cause a sudden transition not to democratic capitalism but to fascism. See discussion in Section 4.

those, who, conceiving of themselves among the privileged, suddenly find the reality of their economic position to be otherwise.

In the deep-structure account of the transition between systems of production, the development of the forces of production of society at a given stage leads invariably to the emergence of contradictions between these forces and the social relations through which production is organized. These relations, which initially promote the growth of the productive forces, become outmoded, and block their further development; the contradiction is finally resolved in a 'synthesis' in which the system is restructured according to a new and more advanced pattern of social relations. The use of the cusp to model this level of analysis is not obvious, but the forces of production and the capitalist relations which organize them might also be taken as conflicting factors.

The development of the former, past a certain point, tends, according to Marx, to favor a socialist system, and is linked to the growing strength of the working class, while the latter acts as a conservative factor on behalf of the capitalist class and system of production. A trajectory similar to the one shown in Figure 3a would symbolize how, after the demise of the feudal order, the emergence of capitalist productive relations promotes the growth of the productive forces, which in turn later outstrips and/or weakens these relations. Again, the region inside the bifurcation set represents the inner contradiction which is generated between the productive forces and relations, and the simultaneous existence of both an actual equilibrium state of capitalism and a potential one of socialism. This use of the cusp is less compelling than its earlier application to the struggle of opposing classes, but perhaps these two conceptions can be merged by speaking of the conflicting factors as 'private appropriation' versus 'social production.'

4.2. Progress and retrogression

As the cusp may be used to represent the transition between systems of production, the historical stages of Marx, from the Asiatic to the Socialist (or Communist), can be shown by concatenating cusps, as in Figure 3d, thereby also illustrating successive instances of the principle of the negation of negation. The figure also suggests the possibility of moments of choice and alternative routes. The motion of the control point is not fixed by the theory, (Thom's or, for that matter, Marx's), and though the general path given in Figure 3a may be the 'ideal type' for dialectical development, deviations are to be expected. The result of the struggle of opposites is said to be, at best, only generally predictable; in any specific case, one cannot foresee the course of events.

A variety of such deviations is possible. Indeed in Turner's analysis mentioned earlier, transitions from stages 1 to 2, and 2 to 3 are, for Marx, relatively unproblematic, but transitions from stages 3 to 4, 4 to 5, and 5 to 6 are subject to 'intervening empirical conditions.' Entry to the cusp region is not actually guaranteed, since those factors which are necessary for the opposition of interests to become consciously perceived may be absent. The working class may simply organize to secure better working conditions but not develop class consciousness, in which case the system will remain outside the bifurcation set, and the possibility of an alternative equilibrium state will not come into existence. It is also conceivable that after entering the bifurcation set, the control point might retrace its steps as the result of internal and/or external influences. A feedback relation may exist in the region of the bifurcation set between the energy function, which represents the relative strength or probability of the actual and potential systems states, and the motion of the control point. That is, recognition of the existence of the new but unrealized equilibrium possibility may strengthen one or the other of the contending parties (or both). Thus, motion towards the catastrophe-generating boundary may be accelerated, or, to the contrary, retarded – or even reversed.

But a system which went far in the direction of change, and was forced backwards towards its initial state, would be unlikely to look as it had in the beginning. Entry into the bifurcation set of the capitalism-socialism transition may induce a 'secondary' cusp to form (Figure 3e) in the 'capitalist surface' to produce a new pair of alternatives: a capitalist system with liberal democratic politics or one coupled to a fascist regime. The sensed direction of motion of the system towards the new potential minimum provokes a reaction, which, if sufficiently powerful, generates the second topological singularity, and a new potential equilibrium state in the opposite direction. Now, reversal of the direction of motion of the control point and/or the erosion – or possibly the disappearance – of the equilibrium surface of democratic capitalism can lead, via a discontinuous change, to fascism. So, too, can the reversal of a transition to socialism which has already been accomplished.

Other variations are possible. There may be random influences, either internal or external to the system, which affect the motion of the control point. For example, where the forces and relations of production are taken

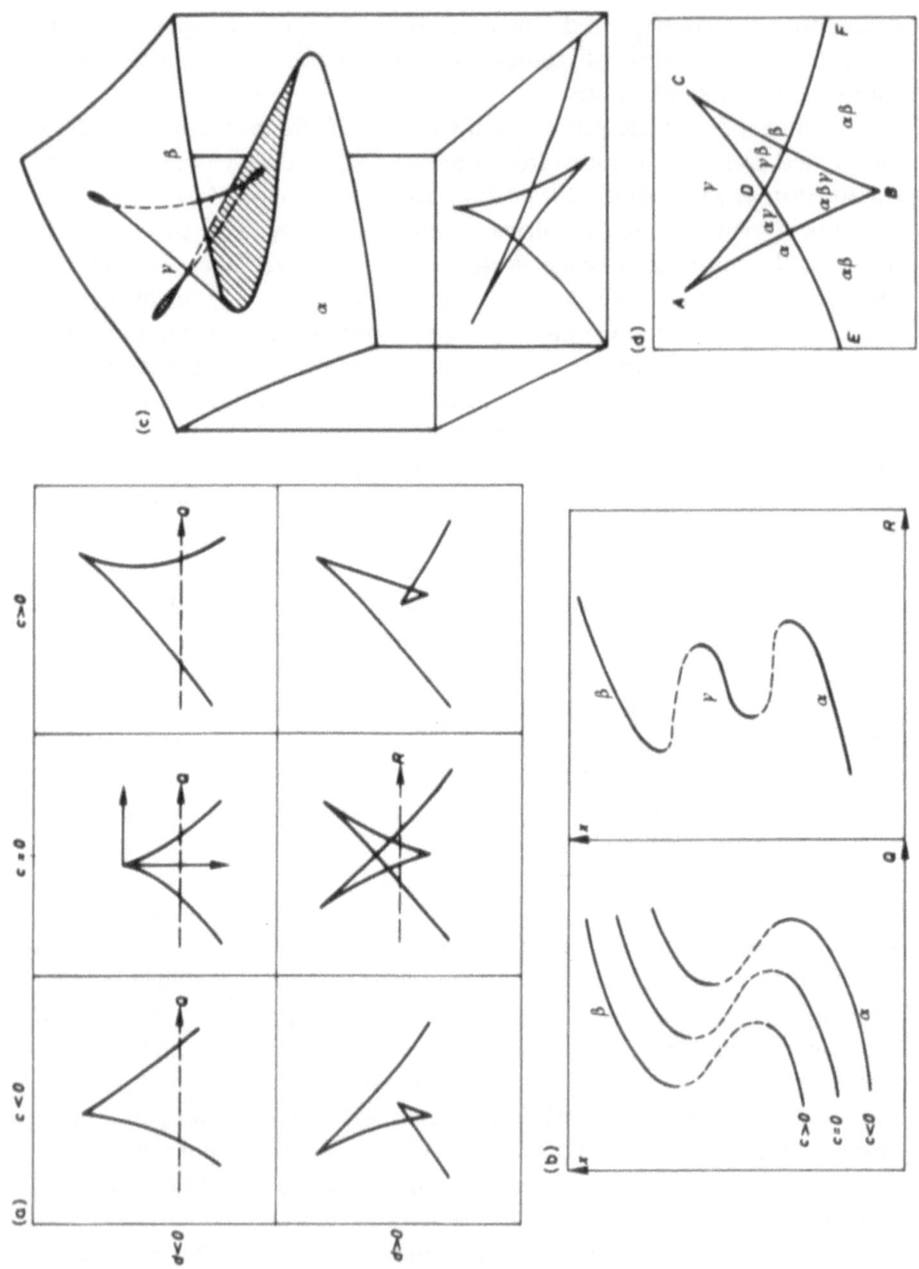
(a)
c<0
c=0
c>0
d<0
d>0
(b)
c>0
c=0
c<0
(c)
(d)
A
B
C
D
E
F

as the conflicting factors, a sudden drop in the strength of the capitalist relations, e.g. due to war, may trigger an early catastrophe, even when neither the productive relations nor the productive forces are well developed (alternative trajectory shown dotted in Figure 3a). The catastrophe theoretic model is only a skeletal framework for analysis and exposition; one may add to it additional features such as feedback, random fluctuations, and so on.

As already suggested, the dialectic does not always progress towards more 'advanced' states of social development. In the critical dialectic of Sartre (Desan, 1965; Sartre, 1977), a different kind of process occurs, which might be modeled as a circular trajectory on the cusp. Sartre portrays how individuals, initially in a condition of isolation and alienation (*'sérialité'*), are impelled to organize, driven by their own need and catalyzed by the existence of opposing groups around them. From a primitive union (a *'groupe en fusion'*) there evolves a true *'group'* held together by *'oath'* (the pledge and commitment of individual members) and *'terreur'* (the threat of the collectivity and the fear of leaving it). The group cannot withstand the need for further consolidation, and develops in the direction of institutionalization and bureaucratization, which eventually completes the circle and returns the individual to alienation and powerlessness. With the formation of the group, the system enters, as it were, the bifurcation set. Somewhere in this process, whether with delay and sudden transformation, or more continuously, the behavioral state shifts from the helplessness and autonomy of

Figure 4. The butterfly catastrophe.

Figure 4a. Sections of the bifurcation set in the (a, b) plane for different values of c, the bias factor, and, d the butterfly factor.

Figure 4b. Sections of the behavior surface for the dashed paths Q and R. For negative values of the butterfly factor, cusp-type curves with two minima are shifted by the bias factor. For positive values, a third minimum emerges.

Figure 4c. Control and behavior surfaces for $c = 0$, $d > 0$.

Figure 4d. Behavioral minima of all locations on the control surface. See Section 5.1.

Figure 4. The butterfly catastrophe. (a) Sections of the bifurcation set in the (a, b) plane for different values of c, the bias factor, and, d the butterfly factor. (b) Sections of the behavior surface for the dashed paths Q and R. For negative values of the butterfly factor, cusp-type curves with two minima are shifted by the bias factor. For positive values, a third minimum emerges. (c) Control and behavior surface for $c = 0$, $d > 0$. (d) Behavioral minima of all locations on the control surface. See Section 5.1.

individual action, to the power and rigidity of collective action. Charisma becomes routinized, ideas turn into their opposites, and the solution becomes part of the problem.

5. The butterfly of reconciliation

5.1. The butterfly catastrophe

The butterfly catastrophe is more complex than the cusp, having four control parameters (a, b, c, d) which affect a single behavioral variable. The new control variables, c and d, called the '*bias*' and '*butterfly*' factors, are discussed below. As before, the first two parameters may be chosen either as conflicting or as splitting and normal factors. It is impossible to represent this form completely in two dimensions, so Figure 4a shows selected two-dimensional sections.

For negative values of the butterfly factor, the butterfly catastrophe reduces to a cusp which is swung in one direction or another by the bias parameter. For positive values of the butterfly factor, the complexity of this catastrophe becomes manifest: the bifurcation set looks roughly like two cusp bifurcation sets, linked together at a third virtex. As shown in Figure 4b, trajectories across the bifurcation set give either two equilibrium minima, which may be regarded as ordinary cusp alternatives, or three such minima, when an intermediate 'compromise' state is added between the other two. Figure 4c shows the equilibrium and behavior surfaces for zero bias and a positive butterfly factor, and Figure 4d shows the combinations of equilibrium minima which exist at all locations on the control surface. Note that the compromise minimum which exists everywhere in the 'outer pocket,' ABC, becomes the *only* possible state in the 'inner pocket,' ADC.

5.2. Two kinds of dialectic

From the perspective of catastrophe theory, the overwhelming emphasis in Marxian dialectics on contradiction and opposition reflects an unwarranted fixation on the cusp. The butterfly catastrophe also exhibits a dialectic, but one in which the struggle of opposites may be reconciled. The previous interpretations of the dialectical principles in terms of the cusp hold as well for the butterfly, since the latter includes the cusp as a special case. However, the additional features of the butterfly catastrophe offer an alternative conception of the second and third dialectical principles. (The interpretation of the transition from quantity to quality is just augmented by the possibility of discontinuous jumps to the compromise state.) Within the bifurcation set of the butterfly catastrophe, there is no longer a struggle of opposites in which either one or the other side must be victorious, but the possibility also of a stable intermediate state. This possibility is absent in the cusp where the intermediate sheet in the behavior surface corresponds to an unstable maximum. The possibility of compromise appears by virtue of the two additional control variables, first the bias parameter which can balance the strength of the conflicting factors, then the butterfly parameter which can induce the creation of the new stable minimum. A volatile dyad is changed into a precarious triad and then into a stable tetrad. The negation represented by the struggle of opposites within the cusp bifurcation set is itself negated, not necessarily by the victory of one conflicting factor over the other (though this remains a possibility), but rather by the appearance of a third stable minimum, which in some cases will preempt the domain of the conflicting minima. Similarly, the triad of thesis, antithesis, and synthesis can be interpreted in a new and simple way: The two outer surfaces of the butterfly are the thesis and antithesis, and the pocket of compromise is the synthesis.

One may object that a true 'synthesis' or 'reconciliation' is not simply a compromise between conflicting alternatives. This is true. Dialectical discourse, drawing upon the richness of natural language, and reflecting the concreteness and context-dependence of human experience, cannot be totally represented within an abstract mathematical formalism. Still, Thom's topological theory does recognize the necessity for an independent impulse which forges the synthesis, in addition to the bias parameter which merely adjusts the relative balance between the conflicting forces and cannot by itself give rise to a synthesis. Compromise may also be reached not gradually, but by a qualitative 'leap,' one no less dramatic than that which characterizes the victory of one of the opposites. Also, in many cases, a genuine synthesis will involve some aspect of compromise, i.e. there will often be some variable whose middle range reflects the reconciliation of opposites. In the transition of quantity into quality, quantity does not disappear but acquires qualitative significance. For example, in the phase transition example, the qualitatively different states of liquid and gas are still differentiated one from another through the quantitative behavioral variable, density.

There are two distinguishable types of dialectic, one which results in victory of one of the opposing forces, and a second which gives rise to a compromise or synthesis. Both of these conceptions have been advocated by interpretors of dialectics. Although the differences between these conceptions had serious political repercussions in Communist party history,[10] they do not seem to have been distinctly articulated, or at least have not gained general acceptance among writers on dialectics. Here catastrophe theory offers the possibility of some clarification. Some dialectical phenomena are best modeled with the cusp; others are more appropriately grasped with the buttterfly. (Undoubtedly, some may call for other catastrophe types.) Considering that the cusp is appropriate to conflict in which either one side or the other must be dominant, while the butterfly allows for the possibility of compromise or reconciliation, the issue of which conceptualization is the appropriate one for some concrete social phenomenon is not entirely academic. Unfortunately Thom's theory does not offer any account, or at least one comprehensible to a general reader, of how and under what conditions it is possible to transform a cusp into a butterfly.

5.3. Synthesis and fragmentation

A 'butterfly of reconciliation' may be illustrated using the account of Curle (1972) of stages of conflict resolution, as follows:

> 'The prototypical unpeaceful relationship is that of a master and slave, where the slave is ignorant of the enormity of his position and of the fact that it could ever be changed.... This situation can be altered only by what I broadly term *education*, implying some growth of awareness of his position in the slave.
>
> Once the slave (or dominated group) is aware, he (or it) struggles to reach a position of equality with his master (or the ruling group) so that the relationship can be reordered in accordance with principles of justice.... This is the stage of *confrontation*.
>
> These two methods, education and confrontation, constitute... the revolutionary stages of peacemaking, whose primary aim is to reduce the imbalance of power.... They are followed by three processes that are more appropriate to equal rather than unequal parties in conflict. By techniques of *conciliation*, hostile individuals are brought to the point where they perceive each other with less unreasonable fear and hostility so they can, with some hope of success, begin the process of *bargaining* which leads to a settlement of the dispute and a resolution of the conflict. Finally there is a stage of *development* in which the negative absence of hostilities is transformed into a positive collaboration... [and] cooperation.'

This sequence might be compared with Turner's description of dialectics, mentioned earlier. It is represented in Figure 5, with some alteration, as a particular trajectory on the butterfly.[11]

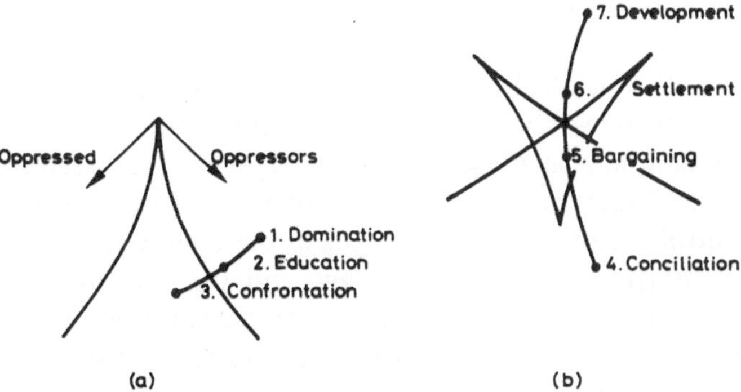

Figure 5. Conflict resolution interpreted on the butterfly (a) Revolutionary stages. (b) Relations among equals. The revolutionary stages are shown in terms of a changing relative balance of conflicting factors, representing the strength and/or advantage of the oppressed and oppressor groups. This cuspian situation becomes transformed at point 4 to a true butterfly as the butterfly factor takes on positive values (not actually shown in the figure.) The trajectory continues on to stage F with further changes in the conflicting and butterfly factors. See Section 5.3 and Note 11 for additional discussion.

The first three stages are purely cuspian, and bring the system to a state of conflict within the bifurcation set. Point 4 marks the appearance of the possibility of compromise, with the emergence of small positive values for the butterfly factor, but the compromise is not actually accessible, since the control point is in a region having only the two cusp minima. In the next stage (point 5), all three states are available, and with transition to the inner procket region (point 6), the synthesis is actually achieved. In the development stage, the risk of catastrophic loss of agreement is lessened, and a continuous range of cooperative behavior becomes possible. However, as long as the topological singularity, and its associated butterfly morphology, do not actually disappear, there is always the possibility of retrogression – either to a state of uneasy compromise or to the actual resumption of conflict.

Indeed, it is possible for the process to run in reverse. A creative synthesis (of the interests of contending parties, of ideas, or of values) which suffers a distortion of the balancing factor or a weakening of the integrating factor may fragment into unreconciled opposites, one or the other of which eventually gains dominance.

6. Conclusions

To recapitulate, the classical dialectic laws can be interpreted using the elementary catastrophes known as the cusp and butterfly. In terms of the cusp, the first law is illustrated in divergence and discontinuous jumps; the second law, in the bimodality of the behavior surface, the conflicting control factors, and the changes in the energy function as the bifurcation set is traversed. The third law, and the triad of thesis/antithesis/synthesis, is exhibited either in the three surfaces of two concatenated cusps, or in the three distinct regions in the control plane of a single cusp. A particular trajectory of the control point illustrates the dialectical concerption that development gives rise to contradictions within a system, which lead to its transformation. In the butterfly, divergence and discontinuous jumps occur between three, rather than two, minima. The struggle of opposites is no longer absolute. The negation of negation and the dialectical triad may refer to either the effect variables of the causal parameters, i.e. either the three equilibrium regions of the behavior surface or the two conflicting variables plus the combined action of bias and butterfly factors. A particular motion of the control point illustrates the dialectical process by which conflicts may be resolved. Both the cusp and the butterfly can display not only the evolution of systems but their involution; not only progressive development and liberation, but also degeneration and rigidification. It should be clear that the qualitative use of catastrophe theory, like dialectics, depends extensively upon the opinions and values of the investigator.

From the perspective of catastrophe theory, both the complete rejection of dialectics as vague or metaphysical, and the claims of universality made on its behalf by official Communist philosophy, are unfounded. A more accurate view would be that dialectics and catastrophe theory are modes of inquiry and exposition. They provide general models about process and are 'systems' frameworks.[12] They are applicable to a variety of phenomena, but are hardly complete or universal. Also, they must be supplemented by concrete knowledge of the phenomena being described, else they indeed dissipate into flights of fancy or rigidify into dogma.

The present paper ranges over a broad array of subjects and is necessarily brief. Many of the topics touched upon, need (and can) be given fuller treatment, and this will be undertaken in subsequent papers. It would be of interest, in terms of the present perspective, to survey systematically – and attempt a taxonomic classification of – the varying interpretations and examples given of dialects in its voluminous literature. The philiosophical affinity between catastrophe theory and dialects could be explored more fully. Thom's aversion toward the Newtonian world-view which emphasizes the continuity of differential equations and the reducibility of phenomena, is close in spirit to the dialectical rejection of 'mechanistic' materialism.

The use of catastrophe theory models in the social sciences is just beginning, and here interaction with the rich Marxist literature might be stimulating to both. One possible quantitative application might be the extension of Zeeman's dicsussion of stock market cycles (1977) to business cycles in general. Most uses of Thom's theory will, however, remain qualitative or even just symbolic or evocative, but as long as *a priori* validity is not claimed for such analyses on the basis of Thom's topological proofs, catastrophe theory will be more illuminating than misleading. Whether truly quantitative and rigorous use of the theory is possible in the social sciences, only time will tell.

In closing, it must be acknowledged that dialectics and catastrophe theory overlap only partially. Catastrophe theory hardly stands in need of dialectical legitimation or interpretation, and a great deal, probably the most socially relevant, and also the most subtle, aspects of dialectics cannot be encompassed within (or even illuminated by) any formal mathematical theory. Still, there is a deep connection between these two modes of thought. In an age inundated by ever-increasing knowledge about ever more minute aspects of reality, one should be grateful for, and tolerate the limitations of, those thought forms which are very general, and which, having the capacity to illuminate individual and social experience, can become also personally meaningful.

Notes

1. Thom (1975) is the author of the theory, but his writings are less accessible for the non-mathematician than the work of his principal 'disciple', Zeeman (1976, 1977). The latter's book contains a host of applications, at various levels of mathematical diffuculty, to the physical, biological, and social sciences, and also a current bibliography.
2. This paper draws upon a variety of primary and secondary references on the dialectical principles (Cornforth, 1975; Engels, 1970, 1973; Graham, 1971; Hegel, 1951; Kursanov, 1967; Marcuse, 1960; McGill and Parry, 1948; Stalin, 1940; Venable, 1966; Wetter, 1958), but it is unfortunately utterly beyond its scope to take up the

differences of interpretation among these sources. The author has made extensive use (especially in Section 3) of the essay of Cornforth, which is a short, clear, and 'orthodox' Marxist presentation, and one in which the similarities of dialects to cata strophe theory are strikingly manifest.

3. The word 'catastrophe' in this paper is nearly always used as a technical term. It is the name that Thom has given to his topological theory, and to the seven archetypal forms which it encompasses. The ordinary meaning of the word, signifying something disastrous, should not generally be inferred, although occasionally it may be appropriate. Nor should the term be associated with any particular ideological position which has been held in the intellectual/political history of dialectics.
4. Within official Soviet and eastern European philosophy, dialectics and materialism are, of course, wedded together, but only dialectics will be considered in this paper.
5. Strictly speaking, the 'control' and 'behavior' variables can have a reciprocal relationship which departs from that of simple cause and effect.
6. Technically, the bifurcation set refers to the cusp-shaped boundary, which is the locus of points on the control plane at which sudden changes can occur in the behavior variable. However, this term is also used more loosely to denote the region inside this boundary.
7. Some mathematical details: The energy function has the form:

$$V = x^4/4 - ax^2/2 + bx,$$

and Figure 1b plots V versus x for the sequence of values of the parameter, b, corresponding to the path indicated for the control point (the other parameter is held constant). The rate of change of the behavioral variable is assumed to vary with the gradient of V, and so the behavior surface is given by the equilibrium equation:

$$\varepsilon \mathring{x} = -\delta V/\delta x = 0 = x^3 - ax + b$$

where ε is small. In the limit of $\varepsilon \rightarrow 0$, return to the behavior surface after some displacement from it, such as occurs in catastrophe jumps, is instantaneous. The motion of the control point will typically be specified by equations of the form:

$$\mathring{a} = f(x, a, b)$$
$$\mathring{b} = g(x, a, b)$$

These are not furnished by the theory, but must be determined for each phenomenon being modeled.

8. This illustrates the dialectical 'categories' of 'possibility and actuality.' Cusp interpretations can be given to other category pairs: 'Essence and appearance' might be illustrated by the distinction between control and behavior variables. 'Necessity and contingency' are reflected in the underlying topological structure of the cusp surface, which is fixed, contrasted with certain geometrical distortions which are allowed; or in random effects on an otherwise deterministic motion of the control point, which make the moment of catastrophe unpredictable, or cause divergence.
9. This is the classic codification of Stalin (1940). The dialectic can be a powerful and subtle tool for social criticism, but this does not preclude its crystallization into dogma or its ornamental use to legitimate a totalitarian order.
10. Deborin, for example, was attacked in part for advocating the reconciliation of opposites; Bukharin also had such a view (Wetter, 1958).

11. The first two control parameters are chosen as conflicting factors, which represent the strengths of the dominating and dominated groups. It is more difficult to suggest the nature of the bias and butterfly factors, but they relate perhaps to whatever forces exist which serve the cause of justice, and to those commonalities, deeper than the overt struggle, which bind together the contenders.
12. The more general affinity which exists between Marxism and systems theory is coming to be increasingly recognized, (e.g. Amburgey and McQuarie, 1977; Kirschenmann 1970; Merrill, 1977; Wallerstein, 1974).

I would like to thank Tom LaBerge for editorial assistance and preparation of the figures.

References

Amburgey, T. and D. McQuarie, 'System Change in Karl Marx's Model of Socio-economic Formation.' *General Systems* 22, 99-103, 1977.
Cornforth, M., *Materialism and the Dialectical Method*, New York: International, 1975.
Curle, A., *Mystics and Militants*, London: Tavistock, 1972.
Desan, W., *The Marxism of Jean-Paul Sartre*, Garden City: Doubleday, 1965.
Dodson, M. M., 'Darwin's Law of Natural Selection and Thom's Theory of Catastrophes.' *Mathematical Biosciences* 28, 243-274, 1976.
Engels, F., *Anti-Duhring*, New York: International, 1970.
Engels, F., *Dialectics of Nature*, New York: International, 1973.
Engels, F., *Ludwig Feuerbach*, New York: International, 1941.
Engels, F., *Socialism: Utopian and Scientific.* Marx and Engels, *Selected Works*, New York: International, 1968.
Fowler, D. H., 'The Reimann-Hugoniot Catastrophe and the Van der Waals Equation' in C. H. Waddington (ed.), *Towards a Theoretical Biology*, Vol. 4, Chicago: Aldine-Atherton, 1-7, 1972.
Graham, L. R., *Science and Philosophy in the Soviet Union*, New York: Vintage, 1971.
Hegel, G. W. F., *Science of Logic*, W. H. Johnston, and L. G. Struthers (trans.). New York: Macmillan, 1951.
Kirschenmann, P. P., *Information and Reflection*, New York: Humanities, 1970.
Kursanov, G., *Fundamentals of Dialectical Materialism*, Moscow: Progress, 1967.
Marcuse, H., *Reason and Revolution*, Boston: Beacon, 1960.
Marx, K., *A Contribution to the Critique of Political Economy*, Chicago: Kerr, 1904.
Marx, K., *Capital*, Vol. 1-3, New York: International, 1967.
Marx, K. and F. Engels, *The German Ideology*, New York: International, 1947.
Marx, K. and F. Engels, *Manifesto of the Communist Party* in Marx and Engels, *Selected Works*, New York: International, 1968.
McGill, V. U. and W. T. Parry, 'The Unity of Opposites: A Dialectical Principle.' *Science and Society* 12, 418-444, 1948.
Merrill, J., 'Marxism and Systems Theory: A New Intellectual Convergence?' unpublished manuscript, March 25, 1977.
Sartre, J. P., *Critique of Dialectical Reason*, A. Sheridan-Smith (trans.). Honolulu: University of Hawaii, 1977.
Schulman, L. S. and M. Revzen, 'Phase Transitions as Catastrophes.' *Collective Phenomena* 1, 43-47, 1972.
Stalin, J., *Dialectical and Historical Materialism*, New York: International, 1940.
Thom, R., *Structural Stability and Morphogenesis*, Reading: Benjamin, 1975.
Turner, J. H., *The Structure of Sociological Theory*, Homewood: Dorsey, 1974.

Venable, V., *Human Nature, The Marxian View*, Cleveland: Meridian, 1966.
Waddington, C. H., 'A Catastrophe Theory of Evolution.' *Annals of the New York Academy of Sciences* 231, 32-42, 1974.
Wallerstein, I., *The Modern World System*, New York: Academic, 1974.
Wetter, G. A., *Dialectical Materialism*, Westport: Greenwood, 1958.
Zeeman, E. C., 'Catastrophe Theory.' *Scientific American* (April): 65-83, 1976.
Zeeman, E. C., *Catastrophe Theory: Selected Papers 1972-1977*, Reading: Addison-Wesley, 1977.